THE NEW LEFT TODAY:

AMERICA'S TROJAN HORSE

By The Same Author

The New Left

Road to Revolution

The Intelligent Student's Guide to Survival
(with Douglas Hyde)

The "New Red China Lobby" (editor)

Poems
Dedicated To the One I Love
(with R. Taus)

THE NEW LEFT TODAY:

America's Trojan Horse

by

Phillip Abbott Luce

THE CAPITOL HILL PRESS

WASHINGTON, D. C.

THE NEW LEFT TODAY: AMERICA'S TROJAN HORSE

Copyright © 1971 by Phillip Abbott Luce

Library of Congress Catalog Card Number 70-179917

Third Printing December 1972

Printed in the United States of America

The Capitol Hill Press, Inc.
1825 Connecticut Avenue, N.W.
Washington, D.C. 20009

Contents

PHILLIP ABBOTT LUCE

In 1965 Phillip Abbott Luce delivered a major setback to the American New Left by leaving the Progressive Labor Party to expose the treachery and totalitarian goals of organizations within the radical movement.

Luce, who holds a B.A. in history from Mississippi State University and an M.A. in political science from Ohio State University, first became associated with the radical left in 1961 when he had a brief flirtation with the Communist Party. As the process of radicalization increased, he turned toward more militant organizations. By 1963 he had become involved with radical elements organizing illegal trips to Cuba. Through these trips he met leaders of the Maoist Progressive Labor Party and was induced to join that organization in 1963.

Under the direction of Progressive Labor, Luce led the 1963 trip to Cuba and returned home to organize a similar trip the following year. He was indicted by a grand jury for his role in the Cuban journeys.

Phillip Luce rose quickly in the Progressive Labor hierarchy. During the 1963-64 period he served as editor of *Progressive Labor* magazine. Luce was also assigned to assume leadership roles in clandestine PL activity designed to foment violent revolution.

By 1965, however, Progressive Labor's strong-arm methods and constant reliance on deceit and violence had produced a severe conflict with Luce's inherent belief in individualism. To help resolve this conflict, he took a "leave of absence" from Progressive Labor. During this period he resolved to reject the ideological falsity of the New Left and work toward a thorough exposure and understanding of radical objectives.

Luce's public break with Progressive Labor came in 1965 when he published, in the *Saturday Evening Post,* an article relating his experiences in the Communist movement. As a result, Luce was subjected to a torrent of verbal abuse and smears designed to cast doubt on his credibility.

In 1966 Phillip Luce published his first book, *The New Left.*

Subsequently he wrote *Road To Revolution, The Intelligent Student's Guide To Survival,* and a volume of poetry, *Dedicated To The One I Love.*

During 1969-70, Phillip Luce served as College Director of Young Americans For Freedom. He has also served as a consultant to the House Internal Security Committee and lecturer at the United States Air Force School of Counter-Insurgency.

In addition to his books, Luce has written numerous magazine articles exposing the New Left. His works have appeared in periodicals such as *The Reader's Digest, National Review,* and *Human Events,* to name a few.

At present, Luce is editor of *The Pink Sheet On the New Left,* a bi-weekly newsletter reporting on current radical activity.

A much sought after college lecturer, Luce has addressed students at Harvard, Yale, Columbia, Stanford, the University of Wisconsin and other schools too numerous to list. He has also appeared on the Dick Cavett Show, the Joe Pyne Show, and Irv Cupcinet's show in Chicago.

Reviews of Phillip Luce's material have appeared in periodicals throughout the country. Conservatives and Libertarians praise his efforts in exposing the New Left. New Leftists, struck with horror when Luce details their activities, will be no happier with this expose, *The New Left Today: America's Trojan Horse.*

ACKNOWLEDGMENTS

I wish to thank Herb Romerstein and Henry Durkin for their help with this book. And I am especially indebted to Isaac Don Levine who made it possible for my first book, *The New Left*, to see the light of day in 1966.

I am especially grateful to Tom Phillips and his excellent staff at Capitol Hill Press for their help in getting this present book published.

This book could not have been completed without the research, typing and invaluable assistance of my secretary, Jane Scalise. Mary Ellen Turner deserves more than a medal for baby-sitting with Dylan through this book's inception and formation.

To my wife Barbra, roses on your pillow. Without her love and understanding this book would still be an outline in my mind.

This book is dedicated to
Mary and Paul Luce
who have the future in their bones
and
to Dylan Abbott-Phillip Luce
who has my heart and my love.

INTRODUCTION

This book means a great deal to me. I left the New Left six years ago. Since then I have been an active witness to the total degeneration of what began as an idealistic movement into the depths and despairs of a totalitarian and 'old' (in the sense of ideology, theory and practice) movement. The New Left now stands as a symbol of all the evils usually associated with the Old Left, i.e., the Communist Party and/or the Trotskyites. The purported newness of the New Left fell into the bear trap of encompassing the same policies and rhetoric of the Old Left.

In the beginning, the New Left understood that something was amiss in this nation. The founders of this New Left reasoned that neither the current political status-quo nor the socialist states, as exemplified by the Soviet Union and its slave states, were the solution to the problems they reasoned were facing the American people. But as history teaches, the New Left fell victim to the power politics of the Old Left. As a result, what is still rhetorically referred to as the New Left is, in reality, only a Dorian Grey picture of the original visions of its founders.

Still, while the initial sparks of political insight as espoused by such as C. Wright Mills have been replaced with the "Quotations of Chairman Mao," the public acceptance and journalistic value of the term "New Left" lingers.

However, what today is commonly called the New Left has about as much truthful relationship with "newness" as the horse and buggy.

As I look back on the birth of the New Left, it is almost impossible to translate the initial emotional and psychological actions of the early 1960's into the realities of the 1970's. The world has moved dramatically and the early, often libertarian, leanings of the New Left have been dynamited by the dogma of the politically chauvinistic machismo of a movement devoted to the inherent totalitarianism of a Mao Tse-tung.

I continue to use the term New Left although I realize that it is an abortion of its earlier meaning. The New Left has interlocked itself with the Old Left. For those adept in mathematical theories the New and Old Left resemble the prototype of the Klein bottle.

Before the reader delves into this book, allow me to state that I am not contending that every young person who is "alienated" from the current political/social system is either a communist or a nihilist. Most of the young people whom I meet while touring this nation are not political radicals and reject the concepts of any kind of totalitarian state control. Many emotionally call themselves New Leftists (although they are not members of any existing New Left organizations) because they falsely ascribe to the assumption that some kind of socialism will solve the inherent human dilemma. The majority of these youthful protestors are idealists who know nothing of history or economics. But outside of the organized groups that I list in this study, most cannot be classified as communists by either instinct or decision.

One final word prior to beginning *The New Left Today: America's Trojan Horse*—this book is not meant as a personal narrative. It is, however, a combination of actual history and personal involvement. It will stand, I pray, as an historical journal of the New Left.

TOTALITARIAN TOPOGRAPHY 1

"CHE Lives." This was the slogan a group of young college students once proposed painting on one of the sculptures at Mount Rushmore. In New York City some young Communists planned to enter the Stock Exchange building posing as business students and, once inside, disrupt the business of the stock market to show opposition to American involvement in Vietnam.

Within recent years, some other Americans have burned their draft cards, signed declarations stating their refusal to serve in the army, rioted on campuses across the country, and fought with the police. Others have proclaimed themselves "Communists," supported the development of revolutionary groups in this country, and openly advocated the overthrow of the American government.

Throughout the United States, a portion of our students are in a state of rebellion against the confines of the political and

1

social status quo of our parents. Irving Howe has written of these rebels: "There is a new radical mood in limited sectors of American society . . . For this disturbing minority I have no simple name; sometimes it looks like kamikaze radicalism, sometimes like white Malcolmism, sometimes like black Maoism." The name that has gained general acceptance when describing this "new radical mood" is The New Left.

Mere description of the New Left is not enough, however, to give a true picture of either what the movement encompasses or why some young people have been drawn to it. I have written this study of the New Left because I believe that my personal knowledge of the inner workings of the various groups involved may serve to expose the many hidden facts behind the headlines. These are facts that cannot be casually ignored, if we are to understand why a significant number of young Americans are involving themselves in left-wing politics.

Parents and "elders" are in a state of wonderment over young people joining the new Communist groups. I hope this study will answer their questions and concern. But it is especially the young person who may be about to enlist his ability in the cause of Communism whom I hope to reach. Perhaps my story will help to convince him that the road to political reality does not lie with the young Communists. If I can keep one young person from wasting the time that I did in the Communist movement, I shall feel that the public exposure of my own political aberrations has resulted in something worthwhile.

The book has not been an easy one to write. For when one has been part and parcel of an ideology for many years, with strong beliefs and ties accompanying them, it is not easily challenged or dispensed with. Nevertheless, it became increasingly necessary to face up to the realities of my political activities since first entering the fray in 1956, to take responsibility for them, and to make some painful decisions about them. These decisions eventually forced me to redefine my political outlook and repudiate the Communism of the Progressive Labor Party with which I had been most intimately involved. The difficult decisions first began in December 1964, when I refused to join a Progressive Labor Party group preparing to go "underground." They ended with the most difficult choice of all—to leave the movement silently, quietly, as so many others had done before, or to risk the censure of those who had once been my friends and tell of the personal experience, political truths, and illegal activities that forced me to "split." The friends who were no longer friendly, the attempts at personal slander, the chorus that now sang out my name as the most dangerous enemy of all, the attemps to isolate me—all were expected. But the contemptuous and defamatory quality of the attacks was not, and the only thing one can say is that the Old and New Left have this something in common—they have no scruples when it comes to one who sways from their prescribed faith.

Before plunging into an exposition of my personal experiences in the New Left, I think it important to define what I mean by the expression, and what particular groups and programs are involved. The New Left of which I speak is the aggressive implementation of Old Left (Communist) ideology among young people.

Affected by this implementation are young people in the established radical parties and organizations: members of Progressive Labor, Young Socialist Alliance, SDS (in all its current factions), and the CP youth arm, the Young Workers Liberation League.

Not included in the New Left of which I speak are all of the voluminous groups that exist on individual campuses and in individual cities for specific and one-shot causes. These groups or individuals may be part of the New Left syndrome but there is no reason to presuppose that just because someone is espousing a political cause with which you do not agree that he or she is a New Leftist. Neither should we assume that a local protest organization is automatically a part and parcel of some "international" or "national" conspiracy. No, most of the myriad of local or spur-of-the-moment organizations are neither controlled by a radical left-wing movement, nor do they necessarily ascribe to the total collectivist views of the national communist organizations.

There are many young radicals in this nation who are not leftists at all. To categorize them as New Leftists or Communists would be a gross injustice. Radicalism and

Communism are not necessarily akin. The most heartening note that I have recently found is that many of the young people who call themselves "leftists" or "New Leftists" are not buying the collectivist doctrine of the established communist organizations. Many such young people are quite simply libertarians rebelling against unreasonable power and authority, whether it comes via established government or totalitarian leftist organizations.

The biggest problem is in distinguishing honest dissent and radicalism from those who would use the first amendment rights of the American Constitution to destroy the American Constitution. This has been a problem since this nation was founded. But today the problem is greater than ever before.

(The New Left was largely ignored by the press and mass media until a succession of events forced them belatedly to spot a new trend. The 1960 San Francisco riots against the House Committee on Un-American Activities were an early clue to the restlessness that was to exist on the campuses, but most people thought it concerned only the political fringe groups at Berkeley. It was not until Berkeley itself blew up in the fall of 1964 that people admitted there was a new radicalism in this country. In fact, only a small portion of the New Left found itself actively involved in the Berkeley scene when it happened, and the vast majority of people arrested there were not young Communists.

(Subsequently, a long list of activities involving various components of the New Left could be documented: student trips to Cuba, marches on Washington, protests against "police brutality," fund raising for the Viet Cong, college building take-overs, the bombing of schools and police stations, the destruction of professors' files and research papers, the wanton murder of a black janitor at the University of California at Santa Barbara, or the equally abhorent murder of a young graduate student at the University of Wisconsin. These events of the past decade herald the frightening changes that radical New Left theory has brought to the campuses and the nation. /

(However, one of the most interesting aspects of the New Left is the fact that so few know anything about it. In New York City, for instance, there are groups of New Leftists who are working twenty-four hours a day for the revolutionary overthrow of the United States. Also unknown to many is the fact that there are now three Communist parties in the United States. One is the traditional American Communist Party, currently toeing the Moscow "peaceful coexistence" line. A second is the Trotskyite Socialist Workers Party, which has made remarkable inroads among leftists within the past few years. The third is the Progressive Labor Party, which toes Peking's line and has been in existence since 1960 although it was only given party status in 1965.

These young Communists are few in number but vibrant and vehement in their programs. Their three R's might well be riot, rebellion and revolution. They are inbred and outspoken. They know little Marx and less Keynes. David McReynolds summed them up in *Liberation* magazine when he wrote, "The New Left is profoundly alienated from this country. It is 'anti-American' with a bitterness which is new to the radical movement." Writing in *Dissent*, Irving Howe described them as "pop-art guerrilla warriors" and then went on to note that the new revolutionary has often very little serious expectation of actually changing society, and so he tries to assault the sensibilities of a world he cannot overcome. "If he cannot change it, then at least he can outrage it."

A more detailed description of the individual groups in the New Left and their programs is presented in later chapters. But before going on to what events and writings led young radicals toward the New Left, I want to describe the atmosphere from which the New Left has been able to draw its recruits. The ferment on the campuses is widespread, the feelings and ideas that led so many young people to ultra-radicalism are not well known, and their attitudes toward parents and administrators are largely unheard.

On nearly every college campus throughout the United States there are hundreds and thousands of students who don't fit the prevalent "accepted standards" of our society. They don't go to football games, join fraternities, take ROTC, or become engineers. These young people and their activities have become of varied interest to their elders, the police, and the college administrators. It is as if the country once again had both discovered and become disquieted about its youth. And it is undeniable that young people are doing things today. Students are involved in every conceivable situation, from peace marches to motorcycle racing, guitar strumming, and gang raping. They have been responsible for "free-speech" riots, jazz riots, panty-raid riots, Fourth of July riots, and the success of the Peace Corps. The young person has been written about, scolded, praised, honored, expelled, jailed, and overlooked, but rarely is he understood or accepted on face value. Rarely is he permitted a relaxed acceptance of himself.

Of course I am not writing about the blazer-clad and Pepsodent-smiled student who quite possibly exists only in the pictures of out-dated college catalogues. I am talking about a significant number of our students who have either joined in some of the above activities or have wished they could. It's easy for the elder outsider to recognize the type known as "bohemian," because of his non-conformist clothing and oblivious attitude. It is not always so easy to spot the fraternity and sorority individual who gets half drunk and decides to wreck a bar or shoplift from Sears. The peace marchers wear buttons that help identify them, but the students indulging in mid-week beer busts wear no labels prior to their act. The young rock enthusiast may wear his hair long, but it may not be as easy to identify the new breed of young Communists.

Perhaps the only thing that all of these young people have in common is a feeling of frustration with American society. Each manifests his irritation in a different way, but all are rebelling against some facet of the complexity, the indifference, and what they feel to be the neurotic ways of American life.

College students, in particular, are often distrustful, pessimistic, resentful, and anxious. They feel like outsiders. They feel separated from the rest of society as they see it "happening" around them, and it is this feeling that was well described in *Liberation:*

> More and more it becomes clear that for all the goods and wealth available, Americans are bored and unhappy. We are led by the nose through our lives, never really making decisions for ourselves, never having the feeling that we are controlling our own destiny, envious of those few who have "made it," the celebrities whose lives seem so

different from our own—so exciting, interesting ... Timid and hostile, we are unable to enjoy each other in the chance meeting, the routine encounter; we pass from our homes to our jobs and home again as strangers never knowing each other, except for our families and a small circle of friends, and we become less and less able to know even them. As we lose contact with others, we lose contact with ourselves; we feel a vague dissatisfaction that something is missing in our makeup, that we are somehow cheated of something we desire, yet we do not know quite what it is.

There are many reasons why college students today are "alienated." One very important thing is that they feel that they are not able to have active control over the decisions and institutions that affect their lives. And they see this very clearly in their relationships with their parents, the school systems in their home towns, and their universities, and in society as a whole.

From early childhood on through adolescence, and in many cases even through young adulthood, they see their parents often acting as a negative influence, constantly criticizing their offspring with "don'ts." "Don't do this," and "don't do that." "Don't socialize with that person," and "don't waste your time with that hobby." Many students feel their parents do not really want to encourage their growth and independence. Many parents, it would seem, prefer a stunted individual who will acquiesce meekly to their rubber stamp. Often parents chart their children's lives like a map, with little interest in discovering what inner stirrings and interests are particular to their child or to the changing times. It is, then, this indifference to a particular expression of a particular person that fills so many young people with rage.

By the time that many young people leave home to head for college, they already feel a sense of "alienation" from their families and from society, although they often cannot express exact reasons for their feelings of frustration. Upon entering college, their frustrations often increase. To that student searching for the challenge of an advancing and exciting educational process our colleges have become a bore. The courses are pre-chosen, the administration has instituted rules and regulations more extreme than the family he has just left, he feels as if he has ceased being an individual, has become a mere punch card, and knows his professors only from TV classes.

The courses gird us for little future work unless we have chosen one of the professions—engineering, or some of the sciences. Liberal arts courses only serve to make articulate liberals. You leave the womb and then the home only to find yourself regulated, controlled, itemized, and graded, as if part of a giant education machine. At home you were at least considered individually, but at college you are a number. Or so it seems to many young people.

It is the young student who feels frustrated, alienated, and angry with the university, the system, and the apparent dichotomy between the theory and reality of our democratic scheme who is usually fair game for the young Communists. The young Communists want to capture these rebels and use their anger for various left-wing programs. Berkeley was once an isolated case in point. The young Communists tried to capture the rebels revolting against the university. It was obviously more exciting, self-fulfilling and politically active to be marching around the block with a sign demanding "something" rather than sitting in the dorm watching infantile television programs.

The young rebel is often both intelligent and active, but not sufficiently challenged by the university to direct his energies toward either his education or our society. Then the campus administrations, usually controlled by our elders, not only play the role of "father and mother away from home" (*in locco parentis*) with a warped vengeance, but also try to control the rebel instead of attempting to redirect his rebellion. The time has come when we should begin to accept the rebel and try to channel his frustration, energy, and alienation for constructive purposes.

The term "alienation" can mean a variety of other things, depending upon the reader and the user. It is impossible to define the term to the satisfaction of all. Alienation is expressed by "being," rather than "reflecting." A Bob Dylan song is one of alienation, while Judy Collins "reflects" on the past. Pot, *Kama Sutra* sex, and bra-less females also are expressions of alienation from traditional society.

It might be argued that everyone is "alienated" from something or someone. The man down the street is "alienated" from his wife, and the women in the D.A.R. are "alienated" from the United Nations. This kind of noncommunication is not as strong as the process felt by young people. The alienation of middle-class students in college, and those who won't make it to college, consists mainly of feeling hate for the way things are, but not knowing exactly why. But if you're black and live in Harlem, then you know why you hate the white man. If you're poor and unemployed, then you know why you hate the boss. If you believe in Communism, then you automatically can hate the democratic state. The expression of alienation of the student is more vague.

What happens when you get to college or on the job and then you find that you are not satisfied? The place where you are is not where you want to be. And you don't know where you want to be. What is the solution? You get strung out. You make love and leave the girl without a word. You cheat in class because you have to. You really can't explain this uneasiness to anyone, because they either "feel" it themselves or they won't understand. Every generation may feel a sense of frustration, but this generation feels it uniquely. And the greatest aggravation is our parents who stand around and tell us how they went through the same thing and "grew out of it." Had they really had the same feeling, they couldn't have "grown out of it." These people claim they were angry like us, but they couldn't have been, because if they were, they wouldn't have accepted society as it is. There are very few "angry old men."

We have rebelled against the system in whatever fashion and manner we felt appropriate or capable of. Some young people take dope, some drive too fast on purpose, others sleep with all the "rebels" for status. The point is not what they do, but simply that they feel compelled to do it. Young people feel that anyone over thirty is an enemy. When you pass the thirty mark, you are not what's happenin'—baby. A few "elders" have made it, but they are so obviously alienated from society that they can fit into the hierarchy of student leaders. Allen Ginsberg, Bobby Seale, Jerry Rubin, Tom Hayden, and now Timothy Leary are examples of this type.

Certainly there is nothing intrinsically wrong with being alienated. In fact, Paul Goodman makes the point often. To remain rooted in a mad society is to become mad. You would be weird if you weren't alienated. Usually this feeling of alienation is submerged, so that people continue to function in society. But often they do not really consider themselves a part of it. The rock-and-roll rioters have their own way of reacting to this, and I offer no comments on them. But what about the young people who have turned to the "new Communists" for answers to their frustrations? Rebellion is vital to a society, but Communism, Socialism, and anarchistic chaos are certainly not.

The writings of C. Wright Mills and the charisma of Fidel Castro appealed to "alienated" young people both on and off the campuses. The New Left concept began to appeal to a segment of the so-called Beat Generation, as well as to the college crowd. Although the glamorization of the "Beat Generation" was founded more by the mass media than by ourselves, there is no doubt that many of us did consider our rebellion symptomatic of a generation. Alienated young people in a state of general rebellion found solace, if not truth, in the essays and poetry of Jack Kerouac, Allen Ginsberg, and the early *Evergreen Review*. No matter how ludicrous their antics and "rebellion against soap and society" may have seemed, or seem even today, to the more elderly and therefore more "mature" members of our great society, they were a part of the beginning of the New Left.

Even today the poem, "Howl," by Allen Ginsberg accurately voices the frustrations now, as then, of a portion of my generation who later turned to Communism.

I saw the best minds of my generation destroyed by madness,
    starving hysterical naked
dragging themselves through the negro streets at dawn looking for an
    angry fix,
angelheaded hipsters burning for the ancient heavenly connection to
    the starry dynamo in the machinery of night.
who poverty and tatters and hollow-eyed and high sat up smoking in
    the supernatural darkness of cold water flats floating across
    the tops of cities contemplating jazz,
who bared their brains to Heaven under the El and saw

> Mohammedan angels staggering on tenement roofs illuminated,
> who passed through universities with radiant cool eyes hallucinating
> Arkansas and Blake-light tragedy among the scholars of war,
> who were expelled from the academies for crazy & publishing
> obscene odes on the windows of the skull . . .

The "Beats" of the late 1950s did more than sit around and smoke pot and listen to jazz and write poetry to describe what was felt by many unable to articulate it. They began to talk about politics and discuss the inequities of the American system and all regimented societies.

The "Beats" struck out against a phony society and ridiculed its educational, religious, political, and economic foibles. Initially they tried to shock society into rationality, as had the Dadaists in France. Suddenly Fidel appeared, and the "Beats" eventually identified their cause with his and became among his strongest apologists in the United States.

A psychologist might explain that the young American radicals were drawn to Fidel and his "barbudos" (bearded ones) because they were searching for a dominant personality to follow. This psychologist might go on to say that Castro and his men cut romantic figures as they overthrew Batista's government with only a small band of guerrillas to aid them, and that they were certainly the direct antithesis of the clean-cut politicos found in this country. The beards of Fidel and his followers were a symbol of personal desire to see quick changes accomplished in their own land. The germ of the New Left was found in Fidel and his revolutionaries, and their cause became the cause of the American New Left.

Just as the student of the day is "wilder" than anything since Prohibition, so the young Communists are "more revolutionary" than anything since the 1930s. They are more romantic than political, and they cover up their ideological lag with excessive emotion. The young Communists are an irrational part of an irrational system.

And who would dare argue that the system is not irrational? Warring Negro religionists kill off each other; a group of young people attempt to blow up the Statue of Liberty and the Liberty Bell; the divorce rate rises yearly; intellectually aware

11

young people are shunted off into the window dressing of big government. We live in a country in which politics has taken on the character of a national advertising campaign, where honesty is rare, where campaign promises are made to be knowingly violated upon election (e.g., Lyndon Johnson's 1964 campaign pledges), where the public has come to accept, and even smile at, the corruption and bribery incorporated into state and national legislatures.

Even with mass media's adulation of "women's liberation," many young women still enter college not to gain knowledge or embark upon a profession, but to "get" a husband. Young men graduate from leading universities unable to spell or know the difference between diphthong and diaphragm. We delight in the absurd, we honor the ridiculous and the mundane, we are discomforted by poets. The trite, the mundane, the absurd, are all symbols of American culture. Doubtless no one would be shocked if national figures, such as Jacqueline Kennedy Onassis and John Updike built pyramids to house their bones along with their contributions to our "great" society.

This is not an exaggerated picture. And there is more. The condition of the world the young generation faces is really too much. If the older generations are leaving this as their contribution to world development, then there is no need for a will. Maybe Edmund Wilson was right when he wrote, "American culture has never flourished; how can it decay?"

Of course not everyone fits into, or accepts, the present image of the United States. There are still thousands, if not millions, of people determined to save this country from the carnival barkers and prostitute politicians. These people, who have seen through the frauds of City Hall and the callousness of Communism, may well yet save us from Moscow, Peking, and ourselves.

Students can no more easily be classified than can adults. Our student population reflects the disparity of regions, religions, backgrounds, and political outlook of our country. It would be a gross mistake to consider students as a monolithic entity. Not all students are members of fraternities and sororities; not all students are affiliated with existing political parties or ideologies; nor are all students engaged in becoming engineers and business executives. There are young people interested in working within the confines of the Republican Party, just as there are students contemptuous of involving themselves in any or all political activity. Some young people major in the social sciences and find upon graduation they have accumulated a mass of knowledge that prepares them for little in the "outside world." Others are so specialized that they appear ignorant of any field except their own immediate preoccupation.

Among all of these diverse aims and careers came a new influence in the 1960s—the Communists. And the New Communists were determined to capture the alienation of the students and direct it for their own purposes and ends.

Of course the sense of this alienation is not new. It might be worth while to review quickly the alienation encountered by our parents. Although the college students of the past may not have exhibited so obviously their rebellion and alienation from society, there is no doubt that they too expressed them in various manners. The young people also attempted to smash the idols and ideals of their parents' generation, and this generational revolt will probably go on. College students of the "flapper" age drove, loved, and drank in quantiative degree equal to their own levels of frustration.

High jinks and pranks on the campus, oddity in clothing, a loosening of sexual fiber, and an approach to politics reflecting contempt for the status quo were always obvious examples of a desire to flout the existing mores of the community. It might also be pointed out that during our parents' college days the major political drift on the campuses was toward the then blossoming Communist Party. Of course, conditions were different then, but as they know, the CPUSA epitomized the essence of striking out against society and its mores. At that time, if you weren't at least a "fellow traveler," you certainly were not "happening."

Today, things are in a jumble. The New Left has gone through so many transformations and mutations that "you don't need a Weatherman" but a program. The New Left has been checkmated on any number of campuses by the growing libertarian and/or conservative movement. You don't see it in the press because these students are not burning buildings or

13

throwing rocks at cops. Still, when it is all said and done there is a strong revulsion to the left-wing terror antics developing on the campuses.

This is not nascent optimism but a hardheaded look at reality. The New Left has received the headlines and the cover stories, but while they were sunning in the spotlights the move towards sanity and reality began to take place on many campuses. You can read Marshall McLuhan and be featured on television news, but you have to remember that ideas and concepts are lost if you are only a momentary image on the screen shouting some obscenity.

It will take time to sort itself out, but the mood on the campuses is not really the radical activism it appears to be. I sense a growing awareness of the validity of certain traditional values and goals, a small awakening of the spirit.

When viewing the campus scene, it is important to keep in mind that the majority of students, like their counterparts in society as a whole, are not political activists, but they are certainly affected by, and take the consequences for, the prevailing political activities of the country and the campus. This is one of the major problems with American democracy today. Far too many of our fellow citizens stand aloof from the political arena and avoid all struggle with political thinking. Everyone takes civics courses in school, reads the weekly news journals, voices support for some political candidate, and maybe even votes in all elections, but that is about all.

People have become less and less willing to voice an opinion counter to the great "liberal" middle-of-the-road consensus. Some concerned politicians and citizens exist, but they are all too often written off as being "over-concerned." The number of concerned parents who daily warn their children not to get mixed up *with politics* must nearly equal the number who warn their daughters not to *get pregnant* before they get the "right" marital prospect. The young person who espouses a controversial political position is capable of producing the same parental heart skip as the one who grows a beard and picks up a guitar.

And by politics I don't mean joining a fraternity or running for class president. The usual parental political advice for a young person about to enter college seems to be "don't get involved"—people may misinterpret your motives; you'll be regarded as weird; you won't be popular if you take a "different" position; no man wants to marry a female politician; you won't get a good job with those outlandish ideas; people may think that you learned those concepts around the house; etc., *ad nauseam.* Heaven forbid that a young person may decide to take a position other than the prevailing middle-of-the-road liberalism, whether on flouridation or on foreign aid.

Most parents pose as liberals, but often act like social conservatives and feel it's better to remain quiet than to involve yourself. Another problem is that while parents may have some political background, they are usually about as adept in relating this to their children as they are the facts about sex. And those who once were in the Communist Party are among the worst. If they have remained close to the Party, then there is a good chance that their children may also join it. But, it is those who joined the Party for only a short time in the 1930s, and withdrew quickly before they got involved on any significant level, who are often the biggest drags. These ex-radicals often behave as if they were in a nightmare world. Believing that they were more involved than they actually were, they have now either hidden their past heresies in the recesses of the college yearbooks, or else have joined the "liberal establishment" to prove their loyalty to this best of all possible worlds. These people disparage all politics out of their own fear.

M. Stanton Evans in his book, *Revolt on the Campus,* accurately and fully develops the rise of the conservative groups on the campuses in the late 1950s. He noted in this study the difficulty of rising against the conformity of "liberalism." He wrote that the "vast majority of college students are probably neither 'liberal' nor 'conservative' in the sense of holding deeply conceived opinions on matters of political philosophy; the bulk of them might be called 'liberals' because the authorities available to them—the faculty, the textbooks, and the mass media—are liberal. They are themselves part of the conformity."

The students of the 1960s entered this vacuum. David

Horowitz, a teaching assistant in English at Berkeley, wrote of this period in his book *Student:*

> Politically, many of us were not naive, but our ideas were in flux. We had thought about the world, about changes it needed, but the corruption of so many causes made us wary of any new ones. We studied society, speculated about its nature, and waited. It did not occur to us then that ideas could affect the world, because politics seemed so divorced from truth and ideals. Our thinking, therefore, remained speculative, fluid, removed. Where, before, generations like us had reached into politics, we remained for the time being, academic, detached, silent.

Into this state of flux come the young Communists. This Communist Left is now actively at work on many campuses to capture the alienated and frustrated student, and to make him or her a pawn in their particular game. "Pawn" is the correct word, as the Marxists and Leninists will use the rebel for their own ends, while pretending their purpose is really only to strike at the evil aspects of American society.

Not only has the rebel been used by the Communists, but he has been misled, if he believes that they have any answers to the problems he seeks to solve. Not only do the Communists not have the answers, they aren't even "cool." In fact, they are usually downright "square." The CPUSA went through its phase of dressing its young members like Sears Roebuck ads in order to dissociate themselves from the "Beats." The young leader of a Trotskyist youth group complained to the newspapers during the summer of 1965 that another youth group was "more interested in smoking pot and experimenting with Bohemian sex ways than in leading the revolution." At the April, 1965 convention of the Progressive Labor Party, its leader, Milt Rosen, sounding like a Sunday school teacher, whined about the "literature produced in this country." He then attacked the "music" and "the girls dancing in cages" as if he actually believed they were imprisoned therein.

But for all of their "uncoolness," the New Communists are winning recruits. Their influence is felt, moreover, beyond the scope of their membership. The amount of propaganda disgorged by the Communists on campuses easily swamps most conservative and "liberal" material. Young people have been drawn to these new groups of leftists out of frustration with the existing groupings and out of a desire to change the wrongs of the system *now*. The Communists offer them a revolution to cure the ills, and many are fooled.

EVOLUTION OF A
REVOLUTIONARY

2

IT was December 1963, and Bob Dylan wove a bit unsteadily as he received the Tom Paine Award from the officers of the Emergency Civil Liberties Committee. Just minutes before, he had succeeded in alienating most of the audience by attacking them as mink-coat radicals, reprimanding them for having bald heads, and observing that he did not see any of his friends from the "March on Washington." Bob then simply took the award, an etching of Tom Paine by the artist Antonio Frasconi, and told the still stunned audience that he was accepting it for the people in the Student Non-violent Coordinating Committee "and for my friend Phillip Luce and all the kids who went to Cuba."

That night, however, more was at stake for me than the financial collection still to be made at the Emergency Civil Liberties Committee's annual Bill of Rights Dinner. In June of that year, fifty-nine of us had packed up and gone to Cuba, defying a State Department ban on travel to that country. When we returned, three of us who went, and one who did not, were indicted by a Federal grand jury for having taken the trip. We were called to Washington, D.C., to appear before Congressman Edwin Willis and his House Committee on Un-American Activities (HUAC). We literally swaggered into the hearing room, determined to give the Committee a bad time. When asked my name, I sarcastically replied, "Phillip Abbott Luce, as in Henry and Clare Boothe." Two days of hearings were interruped by constant skirmishes with the police, when they refused to allow the students in the room to disrupt the hearings. As the hearings dragged on, in the old House Office Building, most of the fighting took place in the hall, where we took the police on simply because they wouldn't let us into the hearing room.

All of us who went to Cuba and those who demonstrated against the HUAC in Washington, D.C., were a part of what has come to be known as the New Left. My own background would certainly not, at first glance, appear to be ideal for any role in an American Communist organization. Born in Ohio of middle-class Republican parents, I led a usual childhood. After graduating from high school, I attended Miami University of Ohio, where I ran track. Then I gave up school (partially as a result of trouble with the college administration over publishing an off-campus humor magazine) and took off to see the South. I returned to school after two years and finished at Mississippi State University, before journeying back to Ohio State for my graduate work. My Master's thesis was a study of the Mississippi White Citizens Councils from 1954 to 1958, based on material I had gathered in Mississippi while working in a printshop owned by the treasurer of the Mississippi Councils. It is popular to assume that most young leftists are "rebelling against their parents," but I seriously doubt that this was a major factor in my own move to the political left.

Although I worked with a number of professors, at both Mississippi and Ohio State, who were oriented toward the political left, they never pushed me toward any political activity. They were not Communists, and the "blame" for my romance with Communism cannot be laid at their doorstep.

Certainly the responsibility does not lie with my parents. My parents took a jaundiced view of my first public radical activity at Ohio State. Although I tried through the years to keep my parents separated from my own political radicalization, they unfortunately have suffered from my revolutionary fervor. Small-town minds can be cruel, and they have, no doubt, suffered for my excesses. Because of their established place in the community, they have had to bear scorn and pain for things I did of which they disapproved. They had no control over my activities and no idea of what I was up to, until I had received the publicity. The only thing I would ever try to redo in my political past would be to spare them, if that were possible, the blight of having had a "Communist son."

I first became aware of the concept of the New Left when I entered Ohio State in 1958 to do graduate work in political science. And the first time I heard the phrase was in connection with the development of New Left clubs and the *New Left Review* in England. The radicalization of my ideas began at Mississippi State, where I was dropped from the staff of the campus newspaper because of my weekly political news column. My attacks on the state legislature and the White Citizens Councils automatically placed me in the forefront of the radical "left" in Mississippi.

My story begins, then, in the fall of 1958 when the civil-rights struggle was in full bloom. Picketing, sit-ins, boycott and freedom rides all captured the imagination of many young American students. Here was an issue of importance activated by other young people. But more than that, the civil rights struggle became an emotional outlet for protest against the entire system that bred the problem. Human rights and constitutional freedoms were considered vital. There was a strong feeling that no one had a right to discriminate and humiliate any other citizen because of his race.

Even in Ohio, which had been relatively free of any left-wing activities during and after the McCarthy era, we began to picket, demonstrate, and protest against the abuses of the Southern governments against Negroes. We also damned the Washington Administration for not moving fast enough and far enough to secure equal rights for all citizens in the country. It seemed inconceivable that Washington did not have the power to wipe out segregation—that is, we felt, if it really wanted to. After all, hadn't Fidel Castro and his revolutionaries wiped out discrimination immediately after taking power in Cuba? We were impatient, and the more older people told us to be patient, the quicker we wanted *all* of the answers immediately.

We simulated the 1960 San Francisco City Hall riots by demonstrating when the House Committee on Un-American Activities released its movie *Operation Abolition* in Ohio. And when the United States "unleashed" the Cuban refugees at the Bay of Pigs, we picketed the State Capitol building in Columbus, laughing off the scorn of the jeering legislators. We demanded free speech on the Ohio State campus and challenged the college administration to try and keep us from inviting controversial "leftist" speakers. Again it became an emotional question of fighting authority. It became a test between us and the administration over the extent of student rights.

While all of this local action was taking place, there was never any serious attempt to unite into a disciplined New Left political framework. We felt isolated in Ohio. We were away from the centers of left-wing political activity in New York and San Francisco. The battles for free speech and civil rights, and the furor over the Bay of Pigs invasion were not isolated experiences. Throughout the entire country, young college students were forming radical new programs. These developed spontaneously, with no set plans, goals, or organization, but it was still evident even then that a vocal and determined minority of the student population was turning to a stronger left in its political development. Students on campuses, even those more remote than Ohio State, were beginning to look to the left for alternatives to what they considered the tweedle-dee, tweedle-dum political scheme in the United States.

By the time I got my Master's degree, I began to involve myself halfheartedly in support of the activities of the Communist Party. I felt that this was the only organization of any radical significance around. I had come to believe that only through a radical change in society could we find the answers to our political problems. Political science courses had taught me that the democratic process "worked," but its pace was extremely slow. As my reading of Marxist literature increased, I became convinced that the capitalist system was bound to create and continue the disparity between rich and poor that existed, and that the two-party political system in this country was designed to perpetuate a ruling-class mentality. As I look back on this period in my life, I recognize that while I was drawn to Marxism as an intellectual concept, I was really emotionally involved in a general rebellion. In the fall of 1961, I moved to New York when a chance appeared that the now defunct monthly literary magazine *Mainstream,* the offspring of *Masses, Liberator, New Masses,* and others, would expand out of its narrow Communist base and take on a group of young radicals as non-Communist editors. This plan was frustrated from its inception, and the "Old Communists" on the staff bemoaned their fate and wailed their fears that "you young people might just steal this new magazine like they did *Partisan Review,* and then where would we be?" The foolishness of holding out any hope for a revitalized *Mainstream* came at a meeting with the head of the Communist Party, Gus Hall.

Hall's office was on the very top floor of the CPUSA headquarters on 26th Street in New York City. The headquarters was formerly the town house of Freddy Vanderbilt Field, who left it to some CP "fronts" when he moved to Mexico. A group of us met with Hall under the most somber conditions. Everyone in any position of authority in the CP had been giving us the runaround for some weeks, and when we finally got to see the "big man," he had not even heard of the proposal to change *Mainstream,* and he had little intention of backing any change at that moment. Added to this bureaucratic bumbling was the depressing atmosphere of the headquarters itself. Hall's office had the warmth of a barren, unheated attic. Empty bookcases lined the walls, and except for a conglomeration of mixed chairs and a desk, the only ornamentation was a blackboard. This blackboard was utilized by the "comrades" whenever they wanted to mention someone's name without its being recorded by the FBI. Instead of saying the name, they would trot over to the blackboard and write it down. A personification of paranoia! Such blackboards, I later discovered, adorn all of the cubbyhole offices at the

CPUSA. Hall's appearance was as stark as the physical layout. As he leaned back in his chair, his feet on the desk, he constantly fingered a clothespin and certainly resembled Captain Queeg a lot more than Lenin.

Our hopes for the rebirth of *Mainstream* were dashed when one of Hall's cronies and apparent chief literary advisor, began to harp on his belief that the magazine should remain a journal to which "a steel worker in Pittsburgh can send his poetry and be assured of having it published."

Following the demise of the negotiations over a "new" *Mainstream,* I began looking for a job. I finally landed one as Associate Editor of *Rights,* the house organ of the Emergency Civil Liberties Committee (ECLC), and had the good fortune to work under Dr. Clark Foreman for over three years. Clark Foreman, whose family had once owned the *Atlanta Constitution,* received his Ph.D. in sociology before he joined the Roosevelt Administration to found and lead the Southern Conference on Human Welfare. He took a leading role in the Progressive Party and then resigned rather than support the "Russian line" the Party took on the Korean War. When the ECLC was founded in 1951 by Corliss Lamont, I.F. Stone, Ben Shahn, and others, Dr. Foreman became its director. He has fought a hard battle to retain the broad interpretation of the guarantees of the First Amendment ever since. Always too independent to join the CPUSA, he was probably the only "old" radical who understood and sympathized with the frustrations and impatience of the young radicals.

Clark Foreman was the only "old" radical whom I knew to be trusted by the young rebels and who opened his home to them. And not only did he understand our impatience, but he often sided with us against the "old leftists." His own independence and flamboyant stance are remarkably akin to that of the young rebel. His friendship, counsel, and understanding have helped to influence a number of young people. Even after I had replaced my civil-libertarian posture with the rigors of Marxism-Leninism, Chinese style, Clark's advice about the necessity of maintaining individual freedoms stuck in my mind and often forced me into open conflict with Progressive Labor. In many ways it was the need for independence, which Clark helped to instill in me, that led to my eventual break with Communism.

Working at the Civil Liberties Committee allowed me to remain outside of the institutionalized Old Left and watch the growth of the New Left. Although the ECLC could be considered by many to be a part of the "old left," I felt the attitudes of Clark Foreman kept it from being taken over by the Communist Party.

During my stay with the ECLC, I found myself involved in a number of controversies, including a duel with my alma mater, Ohio State. I was invited to speak on the need to dispense with the House Committee on Un-American Activities by a left-liberal study group set up while I was still at the university. The erstwhile president of the school heard of the talk and had a mild fit. One hour before the meeting was to begin, he surrounded the law school auditorium with special police to ban the meeting. Although I was prevented from addressing this meeting, the overzealous and protective policies of the president actually worked to my advantage. This lock-out and the resulting free-speech battle became a *cause celebre* throughout Ohio, and I ended up speaking to many more students throughout the state than I would have previously. Had I simply been allowed to speak at OSU, the few stalwarts who might have come out would have quickly forgotten my small offerings, and the whole thing would have received scant attention. I am confident that President Novice Fawcett of Ohio State did as much as, if not more than, anyone else to create a place for me in the New Left circles.

The new radicals ultimately were representing the age-old struggle of youth against age. The young radicals started out to create their own revolutionary ideology, and their overt actions alienated many elders. During the winter of 1964-1965, the elders of Communism jumped on the wagon and began to consolidate their control over their youthful compatriots. While New Left proposals and programs for implementation of totalitarian ideology are certainly more radical than those of the Old Left, the influence of paternal control became more dominant.

These ultra-left elements must first be studied and

understood if any rational counterproposal is to be made. Students, parents, and the public at large must know, whether they like what they learn or not, the goals of the ultra-left and how they wean students on ideologies attempting to transform our government and institutions to an image created by a foreign power.

A number of diverse circumstances have created the apparent resurgence of Communism in this country. The new left-wing movement has concentrated itself in student and middle-class radicals who are seldom concerned with bread-and-butter issues. They are more enthralled with broader ideological questions. Economics, then, plays only a minimal role in the reappearance of the Communist Left in the United States.

Many young people have been drawn to Communism because both parents and society were opposed to it and to their early curiosity about it. The very fact that so few embraced Communism in the 1950s made the movement a more romantic and interesting one for young people searching for something new to expend their energies upon.

Our public image of Communism has also been altered by various court decisions affecting internal security laws and the political reality of the "peaceful coexistence" policy of the United States and the Soviet Union. The Federal courts have gradually come around to the view that Communism is not in itself a crime, and simple membership in the Communist Party does not necessarily constitute treason. The guarantees of the Constitution have protected the Communists and have allowed them to organize and propagandize relatively freely. International agreements between the United States and the Soviet Union providing for a myriad of peace missions, cultural exchanges, and business deals have reduced the antagonisms that the American people feel toward Communism in the abstract. The Russians no longer constitute absolute evil, and their American agents are therefore more acceptable than they were in the past. In fact, because of closer relations with the U.S.S.R., some people now consider anti-Communism a sign of "paranoia."

With Russian Communism representing a more socially acceptable doctrine, it was only a matter of time until the

Communist Party of the U.S.A. increased its drive to gain converts. As American students became more politically aware, they became a primary target for all of the many Communist groups. The rise of the young Communist groups, then, is a result of a concerted membership drive by the elder Communists to enlist those desiring to be "different." Rebellion against parents and social mores, a belief that Communism holds the answers to the future, a nonfunctional democratic left that has left the field open to the Communists, the civil rights struggle, antagonism with our present involvement in Viet Nam, all these helped to drive young students towards the Communist left. The rise of China and Cuba as Communist powers also caused a number of young people to feel that Communism is the wave of the future, and, of course, they want to make sure they will be on the winning team.

The Western capitalist countries, which Karl Marx once assumed would fall into the hands of the Communists, have been the least inclined to show any growth potential for indigenous Communist groups. The only Western capitalist countries to fall under the yoke of Communism have been those taken over by violent revolutions or military occupation, as in the cases of Poland, Bulgaria, Rumania, etc. The only countries that appear to harbor strong Communist minorities are those that are faced with excruciating social problems. Those countries where the major wealth resides in the hands of a privileged few, where poverty is the recognizable essence of the land, where medicine and sanitation are nearly nonexistent, where education never got started, and where unemployment and inflation rise daily, are the only countries where Communism has been the political road for young students and intellectuals seeking answers.

Yet in the United States, where social welfare, education, medicine, labor safeguards, general prosperity, and democratic procedures abound, a significant number of young people are being drawn into the orbit of those who would destroy the government in order to create a totalitarian nightmare. While few would deny that social ills do exist in this country, it still seems incredible that intelligent young students would feel so angry with and alienated from society that they would wish to

27

overthrow it and possibly replace it with something resembling the government of China or that of the Soviet Union. Judging from my own experiences in Cuba and Czechoslovakia, I am amazed that any young people visiting Communist countries return home with their faith in Marxism intact.

In the 1930s, at a time of economic depression and social maladjustments, the rise of Communism was an understandable backlash to the apparent failure of the capitalist system. The young people who flocked to the Communist cause in those years were a part of a system they believed had gone haywire. In those years, it might seem that only radical revolutionary action could save the country from itself. While perhaps not justifiable even then, Communism was, at least, understandable.

But now, by the 1970s, the Communist myth has been exploded, and the social and economic conditions of the country hardly resemble the near catastrophe of the Depression years. The casual onlooker is even more amazed when he sees college students, from middle-class backgrounds, with secure futures, willing to renounce both their schooling and perhaps their futures to join a left-wing radical movement. The usual comment from outsiders is, "How can a young person of his background, opportunity, and education get mixed up with such a movement?" Our Cuban trips, for instance, included the son of a Pulitzer Prize-winning author, the daughter of a leading American critic, at least five children of millionaires, and the rest all financially secure—with the exception of some Negro radicals from the slums of Boston and Detroit.

While many young radicals are not Communists, most feel that the American system has indeed failed many people in this country by not providing them with enough food, clothing, medical aid, social welfare, and equal rights. These young people feel that a country is capable of alleviating the plight of its own poor, if it spends billions of dollars to land on the moon. If the United States is capable of finding a cure for polio, then it should also be capable of coping with bigotry. In short, frustration with the slowness with which our society repairs its inequalities recruits as many New Leftists as—and perhaps more than—an intellectual affinity with Marxism-Leninism.

A variety of young people have been persuaded to join the

New Left, and it is impossible to list all of the individual reasons why they did so. A few cases, however, may give some insight into the types of people who did join these Communist groups.

One young man, whom I shall call Frank, was a member of the Progressive Labor Party for about a year and a half. He joined the group formally after he returned from a trip to Cuba sponsored by Progressive Labor. His childhood years were spent in a university atmosphere, where his father taught. His brother went to college, but Frank himself couldn't seem to make it in the academic community, and he turned to a variety of trade ventures instead. Frank is an accomplished photographer and mechanic, and he spent sometime touring the country trying to find a place in society. He ended up being dissatisfied with almost everything he tried. After "goofing off" for a few years, he left California and came to New York, where he fell in with a group of people involved in Progressive Labor. Frank had a small inherited income, did not need to hold a steady job, and so volunteered his time and services to Progressive Labor. His background in political thought and Communist philosophy was "nil," and his original interest in Progressive Labor was for the companionship provided by its members. He traveled to Cuba with the group in the summer of 1964, less from any really strong opposition to the State Department travel ban than from a desire to prove himself in the eyes of his friends. While in Cuba he met a girl whose father is a leading American literary critic, and they began an affair that culminated in marriage nearly a year later. After Cuba he again volunteered his services to the movement and began to align himself with its objectives. Frank then became a formal member. A sensitive young man, who was unfamiliar with the theories of Marxism-Leninism, Frank was nevertheless a devoted worker and follower of PL leadership. When a "clean-up" campaign started in the movement, he was among the first to shave his mustache and attempt a "new image." At first he was not considered by the leadership as an especially trustworthy member. His youth, his exuberance at inappropriate moments, and his lack of public-relations savvy irritated them. Later, though, he became the head of one of the local clubs and took on more responsibility. Frank is certainly not a hard-core Communist type. He joined the Communist set because his friends were members, because it gave him a somewhat self-fulfilling role, and because it was "the thing to do." Frank was put upon by the leadership from time to time for funds to help support them. During the time I knew him, he was lied to, used, and constantly put upon, because he was considered a valuable tool. One of the people for whom I left PL was Frank; I could not take the responsibility for inciting illegal acts which might involve him without his knowledge and for which he would certainly suffer.

Jo was a member of the Students for a Democratic Society (SDS) while in college. After graduation she had a brief splurge with the DuBois group because she was dating one of its members, but then she dropped out of left-wing politics. She is the daughter of a modestly successful Detroit businessman who is completely at odds with her politics and her choice of possible husbands. Her family relationship has been "strained" for years. Jo studied French Literature in college and became acquainted with SDS when it began a campus campaign to raise funds for Mississippi Negroes involved in a boycott. She became involved with the New Left because of her emotional revulsion from the politics of segregation and discrimination. While in college she took various political stands, such as opposition to the House Committee on Un-American Activities, and support for general academic freedom, when it involved the rights of Communists to speak on campuses. She felt that anyone in this country should have the right to say what he believes—a laudable position, but one based more on emotion than on political understanding. Jo believed that HUAC, for instance, was trying to stifle all dissent in the country and was persecuting only the innocent. She had not formed a clear-cut position on Cuba, but was generally opposed to totalitarianism in any form. She admitted, however, that she was extremely "taken" with the beard of Fidel Castro and "beauty" of Che Guevara.

When Jo left school, she met a young man who was a member of the Communist Party. She attended the founding convention of the DuBois Clubs and later began to work actively for them on the West Coast. She did not attend classes on Marxism, and her overt interest in Communism was limited to her interest in her new boy friend. She ended up on most of the picket lines and was once arrested for disorderly conduct. She was given a suspended sentence because of her age and the fact that she had not been arrested previously. Although she knew from her lover that people leading the DuBois Clubs were members of the Communist Party, she adamantly refused to admit publicly that it was a Communist organization. Then one summer she broke up with her boy friend and dropped out of New Left politics. She then went to work as a secretary in Los Angeles and now considers herself a left-liberal Democrat.

Alex is the son of a self-made millionaire. He traveled throughout Europe and North Africa, and got poor grades at a top Ivy League school. He never was a part of the "smart set," choosing instead to drive his sports cars, motorcycles, etc., with the bohemians. He went to Cuba in 1963 because he didn't have anything else to do that summer. When he returned, he was apparently convinced that Cuba held the key to the future for Latin America and that Communism was the answer to the problems of this country, too. He read little classical Marxism and has only a pragmatic knowledge of Communism. He replaced his carefree life with a purposeful, if staid, political role. Then he returned to school and became an active Communist on his campus. Alex renounced his previous bohemian life, shaved his mustache, gave up various illicit social graces, and manufactured a new image. Occasionally he "donated" money to Progressive Labor, and he seems unconcerned by the fact that if the Communists ever took over he would automatically have to forfeit his financial security. His parents are disturbed by his move into the Communist orbit, but have not disowned him, believing that he may yet "grow out of it."

Bettina Aptheker Kurzweiler was an early and outspoken leader of the DuBois Clubs of America. She has been a member of the Communist Party since her teens and was previously in a Communist "club" in Brooklyn before going to college in California. Although she once denied her membership in the CP, Bettina wrote a letter to the University of California student newspaper in which she said, "I have been for a number of years, I am now, and I propose to remain a member of the Communist Party of the United States." Her father, Dr. Herbert Aptheker, is an old-time party functionary in New York, and Bettina simply grew into her present political role. Bettina, along with a number of the children of Communists, is now playing a leadership role in the New Left. She represents those young Communists who are well read in Marxist-Leninist literature, who are apostles of Communist lingo, and who are outspoken in their defense of the rights of Communists to organize in this country. She is properly appalled whenever the government arrests a Communist spy. Bettina Kurzweiler is only one of a number of young Communists, both pro-Moscow and pro-Peking, who have inherited the mantles of their parents.

I know, of course, my own story best. Since my split with Progressive Labor in February of 1965, I have often been branded a "bourgeois radical," a term of derision among the Communist initiates. In a way, this is a good characterization. Before joining Progressive Labor, I was enamored of the principles and theories of Communism, but I could never be placid enough to accept the restrictions of Communism. At first I found it more acceptable to my own emotional framework to act independently and to formulate my own political solutions.

At Ohio State I read *The Worker* and *The National Guardian* and I often visited Communist leaders when in New York on vacation. When I joined the staff of the Emergency Civil Liberties Committee, as the Associate Editor of their publication *Rights* in the late fall of 1961, I met the full spectrum of Communist and ultra-left organizations. The CPUSA did not, as I have stated, seem radical enough for my independent stance. The Trotskyites seemed too remote and historically confined for my tastes. The other groups seemed even more restrictive, and I never could conjure up any feeling of "togetherness" with them.

When I went to Cuba, I still considered myself an independent Communist determined to raise my own hell in my own way. Immediately prior to leaving, while in Cuba, and upon my return, I began to associate with some of the members of the Progressive Labor group. These young people were openly Communist, apparently unhindered by Communist "group therapy" sessions, (where people met to criticize each other's work) and remarkably independent in their judgment and in their actions. I still believe that at this juncture in the organizational growth of Progressive Labor, an essence of independence did exist. Following the Cuban adventure, the Federal indictments, and the subpoena before the House Committee on Un-American Activities, I began to consider seriously becoming a member of the Chinese-oriented Progressive Labor movement.

My reasons for this decision included my growing belief that individual action against governmental excesses was basically fruitless, and that perhaps more could be accomplished by combining my individual energy with that of others of like persuasion. I was searching for a political philosophy that advocated a revolutionary change in our governmental framework and our social structure. I felt that I should drop my independent role as gadfly. Besides all this, the people whom I felt most akin to at that time were nearly all members of Progressive Labor. I believed then, as I still do, that any serious reading of the Sino-Soviet dispute will show that the Chinese are indeed the true children of Lenin. The documents surrounding the split led me to support the Chinese political "line" and to champion their cause openly and aggressively. I joined Progressive Labor because I had a vision of the future and a hatred for the present. I felt that perhaps a united Communist venture could oust our present government. I overlooked all that I knew of the history of the Communist movement, the purges, etc., and held to a belief that Progressive Labor was really interested in individual freedom and the betterment of the people.

I have since learned how far off base I was in both my political assumptions and my ability to judge the reality of Progressive Labor and Communism. I became a member of the Executive Committee of the Student Committee for Travel to Cuba, the sponsoring organization for the Cuban summer trips. Later, I was recruited to be on the national executive board of the May Second Movement, a Progressive Labor youth and "peace" group. Then I "secretly" became a member of Progressive Labor. The "secrecy" was the idea of the PL leadership, who thought that my usefulness might be enlarged if I was not publicly identified as a member, but only as a "friend." It was hoped that I might, through public appearances and private conversations, serve the organization by appearing to be an "independent supporter and fellow traveler." As a public "fellow traveler," I could always praise the policies of Progressive Labor while denying that I was a member. This policy of "secret membership" is extremely valuable to Communist organizations, for it gives the impression of support from important independent radicals. For a period I even edited the monthly magazine, *Progressive Labor,* unbeknownst to the public and much of the membership. It was not until December 1964 that I was listed on the *Progressive Labor* masthead as editor.

By early February of 1965 I had left Progressive Labor. My reasons for leaving might appear simple to explain, but they were extremely difficult and heartrending to come by. I left Progressive Labor and the Communist world because I discovered that I had deluded myself into believing that this world held the answer to the future and that Communism was basically humanitarian in its approach to politics. No one duped me into joining, and the struggle to see through my folly has been a great personal struggle. You don't discover early some morning that everything you believe in, and perhaps have staked your life on, is a myth. The act of breaking with Communism was the most difficult one of my life.

No single, isolated event knocked me out of the Communist orbit. For those who saw the Stalin purges or the Hungarian counterrevolution from inside the Party, the decision to break was usually abrupt. For me, the road out of Progressive Labor was more gradual, because suddenly I found myself faced with a number of impossible situations. The relatively short time I spent in the Progressive Labor Party saw me rising to become editor of the movement's leading publication, a member of the national coordinating committee, and a spokesman for the PL brand of Communism. Indeed, I might not have left the Communist movement as soon as I did, had I not been accorded a top leadership position and a direct involvement in a number of secret and disturbing plans and actions.

Events within the movement combined to help me finalize my decision to leave much sooner than might normally have been possible. I discovered that I had become part of a leadership actively involving a number of young persons, some of them personal friends, in a series of plans in which the participants had no idea of the consequences. I almost joined a group preparing to go "underground" to carry on the programs of subversion. I was a part of a plan to secrete guns in New York City. And I saw the membership lied to when the top leadership denied that Bill Epton had made his now infamous speech about killing cops and judges prior to the beginning of the Harlem riots. I heard of plans for armed insurrection and was myself a part of one plan to create a riot in New York's Times Square. Intertwined with these were leadership's attempts to constantly deny the membership any semblance of personal freedom. As controls on members became more stringent, I felt an overwhelming pressure to leave. I left Progressive Labor because I could not be a party of a movement based on deceit and illegal activities. My "bourgeois radicalism" rebelled at continuing an association with people desirous of destroying individual initiative, character, and the futures of the membership. I was not willing to sell out my principles and belief in truth to the Communists. I left when it became obvious that the individual lives of the members of Progressive Labor, let alone society, meant less than an abstract Communist catechism as envisioned by the "gurus" of the movement.

Outside the Communist movement, I had based my belief in Communism upon a variety of personal assumptions regarding my understanding of Marxism-Leninism. I had assumed, along with a large number of young people I personally know, that Communism was the most maligned political concept in the Western world. I was thoroughly convinced that most Americans suffered from biased and slanderous concepts of the purity of the movement. There was no doubt in my mind that Communism in practice was totally different from the picture portrayed by its most ardent enemies. The firsthand experience of seeing Communism change the social and political structure of Cuba helped me to overlook and ignore the lessons of history regarding the failures of Communism. My university background had taught me the obvious failures of Communism and the totalitarian nature of the Soviet regime. I felt, however, that our American experience was so different as to allow us to advocate a Communist-style revolution without repeating the mistakes of history. I was thoroughly convinced that we would not repeat the excesses of Stalin's Russian party or the thought control of the Chinese Communists. At the beginning of my romance with Communism, I was a true convert, possibly what Eric Hoffer calls the "true believer." At that time, although I still maintained a strong sense of independence, I didn't believe that I would later come to leave the Communist ideology and publicly denounce it.

My "bourgeois radicalism" led me to believe that a citizen had a right to protest against, and if necessary violate, existing rules, regulations, and laws that appeared to be in violation of the precepts of the American Constitution. One of the ways to discover the broader implications of the Constitution is through challenging various "laws" through court "test cases." Thus civil disobedience seemed necessary, but the "disobedience" was aimed directly against seemingly unjust and unconstitutional acts. This is the best tradition of radicalism in the United States. But the illegal activities of the Communists are not directed at any tests of the Constitution or of the "laws" themselves. In fact, the Communists are opposed to the guarantees of the Constitution, no matter how many crocodile tears they might shed while using its amendments to try to overthrow the government. I felt honored to be able to test the constitutionality of the travel ban, but I was not prepared to accept the suggestions of Progressive Labor that I skip on my bail bond and go "undergound." My own "bourgeois radicalism" was not attuned to the theory expressed by Bill Epton of Progressive Labor when he was quoted as saying that to be a member of PL, "You need discipline; you have to be ready to give your life. This is a revolutionary organization."

I was also not willing to accept the orders of the leaders regarding my personal life or the personal lives of the other members. I had refused to allow the government to tell me how to live, so why should I allow the leadership of Progressive Labor to reorient my life? I had never been organizationally inclined, and the sudden appearance of various puritanical rules and regulations within the Communist group rankled me and led me into conflict with the leadership. Open criticism of the leadership's dictums did not sit well with them, and they immediately began to accuse me of "trying to create a splinter group." I had no intention of creating any "splinter," but my independent character made it impossible for me to accept passively the confines of their Communist mentality. The leaders became so paranoid over the issue of their "public image" that they told members to shave their mustaches, wear coats and ties, forget the cowboy boots, be careful whom they were seen with, stay away from people who take dope, date only certain girls, attend classes regularly, and watch their language in public. Strange concerns, indeed, for Communists who at times attempted to pose as libertarians!

The pressures of the proposed "underground" program, the attempted restrictions on the personal lives of the membership, the prospect of continuing to deceive the membership—these combined to begin to drive me outside the Communist monastery. After considerable reevaluation of my own position within the organization, I felt that I had to leave and try to help other young people keep from falling into the same abyss. My decision was irrevocable, and the frenzy of the Communists at my leaving exceeded all bounds. As if I had suddenly denounced the only "true faith," they bombarded me with invective that has increased in its outrage as time has elapsed. It is one thing to be anti-Communist, but is is another to have left the fold after having accepted its demands. Knowing that I have full knowledge of most of the illegal and subversive activities of the Progressive Labor Party, the leaders have attempted to malign me with the most slanderous and libelous of charges. Borrowing a chapter from the Nazis, they believe that the more often a lie is repeated, the more people are prone to accept it as truth. Nothing is too scandalous for them, and I am constantly amazed at the fact that at one time I was a close associate of people capable of such deceitful behavior. The fact that I have chosen not only to break with Communism, but to expose its operations to the public, has driven my former compatriots into turmoil. The attacks on me in Progressive Labor propaganda have now passed the point of sanity, and it seems apparent that the more I expose their activities, the more insane their antics will become. At present I seem to rank somewhere near Spiro Agnew and J. Edgar Hoover as their most-maligned enemy.

Since leaving the New Left I have been able to come to some conclusions regarding my own political theories and role in society. The decision to leave the Communist movement was difficult, but the decision to join the fray against Communism was not easy, either. Once you decide to testify publicly against former political comrades, you must be prepared to isolate yourself from former friends and allies. Hede Massing, formerly the wife of Gerhardt Eisler and a part of the international Soviet espionage operation, sums up what happens when you make the decision to fight the Communists. In her book, *This Deception,* she writes: "You have lost your first set of friends when you leave the fold. Then, when your battle of conscience has been fought and won, and you go out into the open, you have lost your second set of friends. Now you are alone." You are alone, but not isolated. In the years since I have left, I have found a number of Americans who have gone through the same process of leaving and readjusting themselves to society.

THE EARLY NEW LEFT　　　3

ONE of the first American political mentors of the new era
was C. Wright Mills. Mills wrote a "Letter to the New
Left," in the *New Left Review* of September and October 1960,
refuting the then popular thesis of such American sociologists
and political scientists as Daniel Bell, who coined the "end of
ideology" phrase to show that students no longer were
concerned with politics. Mills argued against this "end of
ideology" idea and outlined the important role of young people
in creating revolutionary situations throughout the world. He
also proposed a framework for the creation of a philosophical
New Left in the Western countries.

Mills systematically began to destroy some of the basic
catechism of the Old Left and noted that

> what I do not quite understand about some New Left writers is
> why they cling so mightily to "the working class" of the advanced

capitalist societies as *the* historic agency, or even as the most important agency, in the face of the really impressive historical evidence that now stands against this expectation. Such a labour metaphysic, I think, is a legacy from Victorian Marxism that is now quite unrealistic. It is an historically specific idea that has been turned into an a-historical and unspecific hope.

But Mills was not simply playing the role of the iconoclast with no ideas to advance once he had shown previous symbols to be false. His "Letter to the New Left" went a long way in articulating who should lead the new movement for socialism.

It is with this problem of agency in mind that I have been studying, for several years now, the cultural apparatus, the intellectuals—as a possible, immediate radical agency for change. For a long time, I was not much happier with this idea than were many of you; but it turns out now, in the spring of 1960, that it may be a very relevant idea indeed.

In the first place, is it not clear that if we try to be realistic in our utopianism—and that is no fruitless contraction—a writer in our countries on the Left today *must* begin there? For that is what we are, this is where we stand.

In the second place, the problem of the intelligentsia is an extremely complicated set of problems on which rather little factual work has been done. In doing this work, we must—above all—not confuse the problems of the intellectuals of West Europe and North America with those of the Soviet Bloc or with those of the underdeveloped worlds. In each of the three major components of the world's social structure today, the character and the role of the intelligentsia is distinct and historically specific. Only by detailed comparative studies of them in all their human variety can we hope to understand any one of them.

In the third place, who is it that is getting fed up? Who is it that is getting disgusted with what Marx called "all the old crap"? All over the world—in the bloc, outside the bloc and in between—the answer's the same: it is the young intelligentsia.

Mills's statement deeply impressed many American students. Finally someone had "discovered" the role of young radicals in the struggle for socialism. Although Mills's writings alone were not the simple key to the rapid growth of an American New Left, he did help build a foundation for the movement.

The Old Communist Left had general disdain for Mills and his upstart theories. The Old Communist Left could not possibly subscribe to the view of Mills that "today in the United States, there is no Left." Only Dr. Herbert Aptheker, then editor of the Communist Party monthly *Political Affairs,* considered Mills' ideas seriously. Aptheker, who sports a Ph.D. in history, is nearly the only *"intellectual"* remaining in the Communist Party. Somehow he has managed to readjust his thinking to the various party shifts. He was elected to the National Committee of the CP in 1961, and it is rumored that he writes Gus Hall's speeches. Aptheker is a prolific writer and has turned out a number of books and pamphlets on the Negro slave revolts and the abolitionist movement. He also wrote *The Truth About Hungary,* a book that defended the Soviet crushing of that revolution in 1956.

Once Aptheker discovered the great appeal Mills had for students, he jumped on the bandwagon and did a brief survey of him. Aptheker's volume, entitled *The World of C. Wright Mills,* does not discuss Mills's concept of a New Left. Aptheker was more interested in propaganda, making it appear that C. Wright Mills was perhaps part of the intellectual community in close agreement with the CPUSA. Aptheker lauds Mills as a "progressive" and tries to align both Mills and the CP as enlightened radicals.

Mills once summed up the New Left and posed this prospectus for the future: "We must stop whining about our own alienation long enough to use it to form radical critiques, audacious programs, commanding views of the future. If *we* do not do these things, who will?"

C. Wright Mills spent his active life as a professor at Columbia University, an independent Socialist, and a writer of stature. It is important to stress that Mills was not a Communist and is not responsible for the turn in the development of the New Left to a Communist line. Mills would not have supported the antics of the Maoists around Progressive Labor or the lunatic fringe elements in the black nationalist organizations. In an article on "The Decline of the Left," Mills made the important point that

In the West, many Leftward circles were so closely identified with

Communism that when Communism was reduced to Stalinism, those Leftward circles declined or collapsed. They had become too dependent on this one orientation to survive intact, much less to flourish.

The case of America in these respects is of special significance because of the enormity of this nation's means of power, because of the *formal* freedom that political and cultural activities enjoy, and because inside the United States Communism has never been a real political force.

The death of Mills in 1961, following a European tour, was a blow to the development of a democratic "New Left." His books still continue to influence students throughout the country, however, and his study of *The Power Elite,* on the interrelationship of the business, military, and governmental communities, is used in numerous college political science and sociology courses. Saul Landau summed up the feeling we had when Mills died in an article in *Root and Branch*, a now defunct "New Left" publication from San Francisco. He wrote that Mills "tried to write on the New Left, but his heart gave out shortly after his return. For the young radicals it was the death of a Prophet. I tried to separate my personal grief. Yes, we felt even more alone now that he was dead."

By the fall of 1958, and throughout the rest of the school year, most of the young radicals that I knew were searching for a program for initiating a New Left in America. All of us were drawn toward the left for a variety of reasons, but we were also completely out of step with the socialism espoused by the Old Left. Not only was I aware of the failures and totalitarianism of the Old Left, but I was equally dismayed by its adopted position of denying its own radical past and trying to pass itself off as a watered-down version of Democratic Socialism. The fire was certainly out in the Old Left. None of the Old Left groups, the Communist Party and its many splinter groups, had significance for us. Their approach to politics was not only "conservative and defensive," but reflected the images of our parents' generation, and it was this specifically that we were rebelling against. Not only was the Old Left elderly in age, but it had already muffed its chance to change the American scene, and it seemed obvious that it should abdicate its role and retire to Miami Beach rest homes. We felt they should open the field to younger and more dynamic leftists.

For the American Communist Party had already reached its zenith. In the 1930s, its membership surpassed the 80,000 mark, but this figure was soon cut when the Stalin purges of that era became known. The CP was able to forestall much of the mass exodus by members until after the beginning of the Great War against Nazism, but by the time Hitler invaded Russia, the period of mass participation in the Party was over. The insane purges of Stalin, coupled with the American CP support of Nazi Germany against the "imperialist" powers of England and France, drove the more rational "comrades" out of the party. George Dell, Granville Hicks, and Max Eastman are only a few who left the party during this period. Eastman was called an agent of the British Secret Service by the *Daily Worker.* He sued them for slander and won a settlement and a retraction. It was this period of insanity that caused Edmund Wilson to recommend that Communism be taken away from the Communists.

By the time of the 20th Party Congress in 1956, when Khrushchev made his historic speech revealing a portion of the heinous crimes of Stalin, while conspicuously leaving out his own part in these events, the American party had dwindled to about 10,000 members. The American people had long before seen through the tactical gyrations and philosophical gibberish of the Communists.

The young people who were ultimately to form the New Left began appearing on the scene in the 1950s and the early 1960s. They were predisposed to shun the elders of the American CP and strike out on their own for solutions to the problems of American life.

In 1960 the young intellectuals in England had also discovered that the Old Left held no future. In January of 1960, a new magazine appeared there called *New Left Review,* which editorialized in the first issue:

> We are convinced that politics, too narrowly conceived, has been a main cause of the decline of socialism in this country, and one of the reasons for this disaffection from socialist ideas of young people in

particular. The humanist strengths of socialism—which are the foundations for a genuinely popular socialist movement—must be developed in cultural and social terms, as well as in economic and political. What we need now is a language sufficiently close to life—all aspects of it—to declare our discontent with "that same order."

Although hampered by its graduate-school approach to the political revolution, the editors of this new magazine at least recognized the fact that the old Marxist platitudes and heavily coined language held no truths for young people struggling to find socialist answers. The early issues of the *New Left Review,* possessed a vital and fresh approach that spread to the United States and influenced a growing number of young people on the campuses.

Although the New Left has now come to identify itself more and more with the precepts and ideology of the elders of Communism, it still holds some hostility for its forebears. David McReynolds summed it up in an article in the August 1965 *Liberation:* "The New Left is filled with hostility toward the adult world . . . The New Left is not only hostile to adults, it is hostile to ideology." But the New Left began to change its tune and shortly represented a new amalgam of groups that were openly and aggressively Communist in nature and program. The New Left began losing its "newness" and became more and more a mere radical outcropping of the Old Left. C. Wright Mills was replaced by Mao, and the prospect of free men acting rationally to change society became infused with and then replaced by the concept of revolution and armed conflict. Not only did the ideology begin to change, but the very nature of the groups involved also changed. No longer do we still see the anarchistic approach of the young radicals to individual social problems. All this has been replaced by a controlled logic that strongly resembles the editorials in the Chinese Communist weekly, *The Peking Review.*

Others who became interested in the formation of a New Left formed around the publication *Studies on the Left,* which was founded in the fall of 1959 at the University of Wisconsin by a group of young radical graduate students. *Studies* has since dissolved, but some of the original editors are now to be found writing for *Socialist Revolution,* published in San Francisco. Although academic in its approach to Marxism and the radical movement in America, this journal expressed the views of the emerging New Left. And although the radical New Left has since outdistanced the journal in its ideas, it was highly respected on the New Left spectrum. The very nature of its anti-American line made it valuable to any young person advocating a revolutionary approach. The first editorial in *Studies,* entitled "The Radicalism of Disclosure," attacked the supposed "objective" position of the American academic and notes that:

> There is work for the radical scholar, the thinker who is committed to the investigation of the origins, purposes and limitations of institutions and concepts, as well as for the conservative or liberal scholar who is committed to their efficent maintenance and improvement. There is room in scholarship for the application of reason to the *reconstruction* of society, as well as to legalistic interpretation and reform. There is a place for the scholar who looks upon traditional formulations, theories, structures, even "facts" with a habitually critical attitude stemming from his distaste for things as they are and from his distrust of the analyses of those who are committed to the maintenance of the status quo.
>
> There is a place for him because, if he is a scholar as well as a malcontent, an honest researcher as well as a radical, his very partisanship, bias, call it what you will—gives him a kind of objectivity. Because he stands opposed to established institutions and conventional conceptions, the radical scholar possesses an unconcern for their safety or preservation which enables him to carry inquiry along paths where the so-called "objective" conservative or liberal scholar would not care to tread . . .
>
> We hope that the radicalism of what is disclosed, as it increases and matures, may provide knowledge and theory for the future growth of a radicalism of what is proposed.

Studies went through many changes and it flip-flopped around on a number of issues concerning totalitarian Communism in left-wing movements. In the Spring 1965 issue, the journal had two editorials that help explain its position at that time. In one editorial the editors note that:

> The issue which divides *Studies* editors . . . is the inevitable issue

of agency: which sectors of American society, alone or in coalition, are capable of transforming society by replacing American capitalism with a more humane set of economic, social and political institutions. The issue is crucial to the continued development of that radicalism variously styled "the New Left" or "the movements"; the division among the *Studies* editors is important because the positions taken reflect not only disagreement but the different kinds of work which follow from those positions . . . The choice the editors made, when *Studies* moved to New York City, was to attempt to engage in a dialogue with the new activists, to seek to become useful to the new radicals . . .

In another *Studies* editorial, they go on to say that PL is part of the new insurgency and we shouldn't encourage the continuation of the isolation it has suffered on the left so far. "We urge our readers to support the PLP's defense efforts . . . ," they wrote.

When *Studies* first appeared, the voice of the New Left centered primarily on Fidel Castro's achievement and the writings of C. Wright Mills. The publication of *Listen, Yankee* by Professor Mills helped to mold the New Left's approach to Cuba. This book attempted to portray the ideas and feelings of the revolutionaries as expressed to Mills during an extensive tour of the island he made in 1960. The message came across powerfully:

> Today the revolution is going on in Cuba. Tomorrow—not next year—it is going to be going on elsewhere. A revolution like ours does not come about just because anyone wants it . . . We don't take satisfaction in the fact that we are the center of the cold war in the Caribbean. We don't like the cold war anywhere—who does? But we are glad, we have to be glad, that finally many things that must be done are now being done in Cuba.
>
> So what can we say to you to make you understand?
>
> Can we say: Become aware of our agonies and our aspirations? If you do it will help you to know what is happening in the world you are living in. Take Cuba as the case; in terms of it rethink who you are, American.
>
> What does Cuba mean?
>
> It means another chance for you.

Mills summed up the New Left case for Cuba. We all agreed

that Cuba was not Communist, but simply anti-American. At this period, we believed Paul Sweezy and Leo Huberman when they wrote in *Cuba: Anatomy of a Revolution,* that "Fidel has explained his own and his government's position on this many times: They are not Communists . . ."

Next came Robert Williams, and his influence on the development of the Communist New Left cannot be minimized. When Robert Williams returned to Monroe, N. C., following a stint in the Marines during World War II, he felt that the NAACP was, for all intents and purposes, a dead organization. Williams took over the quiescent leadership of the Monroe NAACP and appealed to the young people of the community to join with him and revitalize the local chapter. He appealed primarily to poorer Negroes, and although at least one local doctor was involved in the organization, the Monroe branch of the NAACP lacked the affluence enjoyed by most other chapters.

Williams, impressed by a visit to revolutionary Cuba, became an active member of the Fair Play for Cuba Committee. As editor of a small newspaper, Williams soon became a darling of the New Left. He stood against the placid policies of the NAACP leadership and the Old Left, by advocating violence couched in the phrase "self-defense."

Williams simply articulated the demands and frustrations of the black nationalists. He once wrote in the pacifist magazine *Liberation:*

> We live in a perilous time in America, and especially in the South. Segregation is an expensive commodity, but liberty and democracy, too, have their price. So often the purchase check of democracy must be signed in blood. Someone must be willing to pay the price, despite the scoffs from the Uncle Toms. I am told that patience is commendable and that we must never tire of waiting, yet it is instilled at an early age that men who violently and swiftly rise to oppose tyranny are virtuous examples to emulate. I have been taught by my government to fight, and if I find it necessary I shall do just that. All Negroes must learn to fight back, for nowhere in the annals of history does the record show a people delivered from bondage by patience alone.

Williams' policies were too much for the leadership of the

NAACP, and he and his chapter were finally suspended from the national organization. During a 1961 riot over the "freedom riders" who had bused to Monroe, Williams was accused of kidnapping a white couple and holding them hostage. As a result, Williams fled to Cuba with his wife and two children. While living in exile in Cuba, Williams lost all perspective on the racial question in the United States. His publication *The Crusader,* was printed "privately" in Cuba, and sent into the United States through the Fair Play for Cuba offices in Canada. Its violent tone can be grasped by quoting from a sample issue:

We prefer peaceful negotiations, but our oppressors have proved to us that they are not susceptible to such mild pressures for reform and that they will utilize massive violence to attempt to contain our struggle. When massive violence comes, the U.S.A. will become a bedlam of confusion and chaos. The factory workers will be afraid to venture out on the streets to report for their jobs. The telephone workers and radio workers will be afraid to report. All transportation will grind to a complete standstill. Property will be damaged and expensive buildings will be reduced to ashes. Essential pipe lines will be severed and blown up and all manner of sabotage will occur. Violence and terror will spread like a firestorm. A clash will occur inside the armed forces. At U.S. military bases around the world local revolutionists will side with Afro GI's. Because of the vast area covered by the holocaust, U.S. forces will be spread too thin for effective action. U.S. workers, who are caught on their jobs, will try to return home to protect their families. Trucks and trains will not move the necessary supplies to the big urban centers. The economy will fall into a state of chaos . . .

The new concept of revolution defies military science and tactics. The new concept is lightning campaigns conducted in highly sensitive urban communities and spreading to the farm areas. The old method of guerrilla warfare, as carried out from the hills and countryside, would be ineffective in a powerful country like the U.S.A. Any such force would be wiped out in an hour. The new concept is to huddle as close to the enemy as possible so as to neutralize his modern and fierce weapons. The new concept creates conditions that involve the total community, whether they want to be involved or not. It sustains a state of confusion and destruction of property. It dislocates the organs of harmony and order and reduces the central power to the level of a helpless, sprawling octopus. During the hours of the day sporadic rioting takes place and massive sniping. Night brings all-out warfare, organized fighting, and unlimited terror against the oppressor and his forces. Such a campaign will bring an end to oppression and social injustice in the U.S.A. in less than 90 days and create the basis for the implementation of the U.S. Constitution with justice and equality for all people . . .

The handwriting is already on the wall. Victory is now within our reach. LET US PREPARE TO SEIZE IT!

In addition, Willaims broadcast daily radio diatribes from Cuba aimed at Southern blacks. Known as "Radio Free Dixie," Williams' program constantly urged black people to take up arms.

The Monthly Review pointed out that this "apocalyptic vision of violence may be nothing but a terrible nightmare," but there is solid evidence indicating that Williams' "philosophy" has made a serious impact on various segments of the New Left. Three members of the so-called "Black Liberation Front," who planned to blow up the Statue of Liberty and were foiled only because they confided to an undercover police agent, were disciples of Robert Williams. The leader of the group had extensive conversations with Williams in Cuba during the summer of 1964. Another member of the "Black Liberation Front" had earlier been a member of the Monroe Defense Committee, an organization formed to defend Williams against the authorities in North Carolina. "The Black Liberation Front" was, in fact, formed in Cuba in 1964 by the black nationalists who were members of the second "student" trip to that island. There is no doubt that the thinking of Williams helped to mold the violent plans of this group. The Progressive Labor people have also worked with Williams, and they set up a self-defense guard in Monroe after Williams had to flee. Progressive Labor has never hidden its admiration for Williams' advocacy of violence. Williams is an ardent follower of the Chinese Communists. He has traveled to China at least twice and has written extensively in support of the Chinese doctrine of violent world revolution. Following their first A-bomb test, Williams wrote from China that "the bomb is not just a Chinese bomb, it is a freedom bomb."

Williams apparently had some misgivings about the beauty

and peace offered him under Communism, for he returned to the United States. For a while Williams was the nominal leader of a black militant organization known as the "Republic of New Africa."

This organization holds that cooperation between black and white radicals is not possible. Williams apparently modified his support of this doctrine, for he subsequently left the group.

The magazines *Studies on the Left* and *New Left Review* helped break student radicals out of the past, but they cannot be held responsible for what later developed. Although some Democratic Socialist groups did develop from the ferment of the early 60s, such as the Students for a Democratic Society, the unfortunate fact is that this period gave rise also to a dangerous left-wing lunatic fringe. The revolutionary New Left grew out of the alienation and political naivete of young people searching for simple answers to complex questions. Misreadings of Mao Tsu-tung and Che Guevara also did much to create the hydra-headed monster the New Left has become. Although Cuba, which was once the Mecca of the early New Left, has been replaced by a turn toward the Orient and the Chinese Communists, it has continued to serve as an impetus for revolutionary ideas.

CUBA

4

THE great appeal of the Cuban Revolution for my generation of the New Left was similar in many respects to the appeal the Russian Revolution held for the generation of my parents. Of course those older and wiser than we know of the pitfalls of Communism and revolution. They know all about the purges, the splits, the faded hopes. For us, however, the past held few lessons. At the time of the Cuban Revolution, we were not concerned with the past.

One of the most important characteristics of the New Left is its complete lack of information about, or concern for, the debates and squabbles that devoured the old left wing. The freshness with which we approached the Cuban Revolution approximated the naivete with which the American radicals experienced the Russian Revolution.

To the young American radical who was alienated from his school and family and the two-party system, the advent of Fidel

Castro in Cuba heralded hope for the hemisphere. At that time, 1958-1961, our awareness that Fidel was a Communist did not undermine our support. The romantic ideas of, and atmosphere surrounding, Fidel, Che, and Camillo in Cuba seemed to reflect our deepest feelings, desires, and hopes. The overthrow of Batista by a band of rebels who resembled Brando in *Viva Zapata* easily captured our imaginations, and Fidel and comrades became the most appealing political figures since the demise of Lenin and Trotsky.

The appeal of Fidel is difficult to explain to anyone who does not feel it or immediately recognize it. LeRoi Jones, the black revolutionary poet and playwright, caught the sense of this appeal by noting that if you just compared the physiognomy of the Cuban leaders with that of Lyndon Johnson and Adlai Stevenson, there is no question whom you would have to trust.

And don't kid yourself. The beards, the bandoliers, the Jeeps racing through Havana with men shooting in the air, the fact that David had again slain Goliath in Cuba, all burgeoned into a pro-Cuban, anti-American drive among the young rebels who were looking for a radical cause to join.

When the State Department banned travel to that island in December of 1960, we wept. And later, when John Kennedy sanctioned the abortive Bay of Pigs invasion, and Adlai Stevenson led the liberals down the road of lies in the United Nations and was left holding the bag when it was all over, we felt shame at being associated with such a government. C. Wright Mills summed up our feelings in a telegram he sent from Europe to a Fair Play for Cuba rally in San Francisco. "Kennedy and Co. have returned to barbarism. Schlesinger and Co. have disgraced us intellectually and morally. I feel a desperate shame for my country. Sorry I cannot be with you. Were I physically able to do so, I would at this moment be fighting alongside Fidel Castro."

Certainly the frustration we felt with society was accelerated by the Kennedy Administration's attack on Cuba. We may have been naive, but after the Bay of Pigs, many of us felt that we would have real change in this country only with a revolution.

We were searching for something better, and we thought we had found it in Cuba.

At the time of the Bay of Pigs invasion, the American Communist Party finally began to realize that the Cuban Revolution was a cause through which it might arouse and recruit the youth of this country. Suddenly a number of articles appeared informing us of the Cuban CP's crucial role in the Revolution, and the equally crucial role of the American CP as the main defender of the Cuban Revolution here. An old-time Cuban Communist Party leader was given the task of rewriting the history of the Cuban CP from 1953 to 1960. Blas Roca, once in charge of the Cuban CP, and now editor of the Cuban government paper *Hoy*, gave a good account of himself and tried to credit the Cuban CP with a major part in the Revolution in his book *The Cuban Revolution*. The old American Communist, Joe North, came out of literary retirement to write *Cuba: Hope of a Hemisphere*, another apology for the Cuban CP's support of Batista prior to its discovery that Fidel's chances for success were great.

The ease with which we discussed and simplemindedly accepted the Communist coup in Cuba underlies our own failure to understand Communism or its history. The New Left generation was not a part of the early discourse over Stalinism, the Soviet-Nazi Pact, the purge of Lovestone, etc., and we were too much caught up in the movement of our own cause to study this early history. Many of us studied more Marxist classics in college than we ever did later while members of any of the groups presently composing the New Left.

The formation of the U.S. Fair Play for Cuba Committee in 1960 was one of the first attempts to organize the New Left. In the early years of the FPCC, it drew the embryonic left together in a non-Communist organization that advocated support for Fidel against the United States. When the FPCC was formed, many of the people associated with it were not associated with the American Communist left and represented, instead, the mainstream of thinking among young radicals on the campuses.

The Fair Play for Cuba Committee ultimately succumbed to domination by the Old Left Trotskyite Socialist Workers Party and was out of business by 1963. But through 1960-1961 this organization became a sounding board for the New Left and helped mobilize it into a movement. At that time the FPCC was the only organization that responded to the fervor and political anarchy of student radicals. FPCC ran trips to Cuba for about $100 a person, with the Cubans picking up the rest of the tab. These trips were usually dominated by younger people who were traveling to Cuba with the same enthusiasm as John Reed had earlier, going to Moscow.

When these young people arrived in Cuba, they were confronted with the reality of the romantic image they had conjured up. At that time the revolutionaries still had their long hair, their beards, their crossed bandoliers, and their berets. All Cuba seemed in the throes of a carnival-revolution. The young people who traveled to Cuba on these trips, or those sponsored by the left-wing newspaper *The National Guardian*, returned to the United States with the conviction that the Cubans had found *the* answer to the problems of Latin America and perhaps of the United States also. The Cubans had shown that they could oust American "imperialism" and could introduce radical economic measures that might perhaps eradicate some of the poverty so widespread in Latin America. Many of these young Americans also began picturing themselves as leaders of a revolution in the United States that would correspond with that of Cuba. The Cubans had shown us that "bourgeois democratic elections" were not the answer to immediate problems. For those of us demanding immediate solutions to society's problems, only a revolution seemed practical.

The young people around the FPCC, and those who had gone to Cuba to find the truth, returned to unite in their mutual identification with the Cubans and their Revolution. No longer were we individual voices in the political forest.

It was not until spring, 1963, that I became involved in any organizational leadership with the New Left, or more specifically with the New Communists. Following an Emergency Civil Liberties Committee meeting, I was approached by Levi Laub, a member of Progressive Labor, who told me that LeRoi Jones, the black militant poet and political power in Newark, New Jersey, had suggested that Laub talk with me about a proposed trip to Cuba. I was immediately struck with the brashness and boldness of the idea.

Since Fidel Castro had taken power, Cuba was the one place that I most wanted to see. After the Revolution I considered myself a "Fidelista," and I was chock-full of romantic images about the country and the Revolution. Good friends of mine had visited Cuba in December of 1960, right before the State Department instituted its "travel ban." I had planned to go myself the following spring, but after the State Department edict, my plans fell through. Now Levi Laub was proposing that I join a group going to Cuba in spite of, if not because of, the State Department restrictions. I jumped at the opportunity.

I not only felt a political sympathy for Cuba and the Revolution, but here again was the old problem of some bureaucrats telling me, let alone all of the American people, where they could, or could not, travel. This seemed a perfect opportunity not only to see Cuba, but to strike out against the system. Many of the original fifty-nine who went to Cuba did so in part because of their anger at being told they couldn't go. The organizers of the trip had different reasons for sending us to Cuba.

But no matter what the underlying reasons, or the propaganda value to the Cubans, the trip was definitely a blow to the attempts of the Department of State to stop all travel to Cuba. The summer jaunt not only allowed us to see with our own eyes what was happening in Castro's land, but it forced the government into taking criminal action against us to dissuade others from going there also.

Once Levi Laub outlined the trip to me, I anxiously devoted the next few weeks to helping him prepare for this adventure. After an interview, and an acceptance of my application, I became the press chairman of the group. When we left, we issued a press statement I wrote saying in part that "We are traveling to Cuba despite State Department press releases and public notices attempting to limit the travel of American citizens, because we consider it our right to travel where we want and when we want."

The operations for the Cuban trips were like a mixture of Mission Impossible and Jonathan Winters. The results included thirteen Federal indictments, two House Un-American Activities Committee hearings, a number of recruits for Progressive Labor, considerable propaganda for the Cubans, and a black eye for the State Department.

The trips were conceived by Fred Jerome and Milt Rosen, of PL, as a recruitment tactic and a way to capture the spotlight through dramatic action. Individual travel to Cuba had been thwarted since the State Department rules passports invalid for travel to that island. Since that time, only newsmen have been granted exception by the State Department.

In 1963, however, there was considerable doubt if the State Department edicts amounted to "law." The various criminal statutes relating to travel outside of this country were not only vague, but apparently unrelated to travel to Cuba by an American with a valid passport. We assumed that a serious constitutional question was involved here.

But the question of constitutionality did not interest the Progressive Labor leadership. If the constitutional question was their concern, they could have tested the law with Levi Laub alone, without endangering the other people who went along in the summer of 1963. No, Progressive Labor was interested in using these trips for publicity, for recruitment, and for taking direct action against the American government.

For the Cubans, on the other hand, free travel was vital. Few Latin American countries allow their citizens to visit Cuba, because of the terrorist training schools on that island. At meetings of the Organization of American States, the United States has taken the lead in opposing travel to Cuba, because of the threat to the security of the hemisphere that the government feels such travel might involve.

It was, therefore, a tremendous propaganda coup when the Cubans discovered that a group of Americans wanted to break the "travel ban" and come to Cuba. This act would make it impossible for the representative from the United States to condemn any other nation at the OAS for allowing its citizens to travel to Cuba. After all, the U.S. couldn't even stop its own citizens from going there.

The leadership of Progressive Labor had already developed extensive ties with the Castro government. Fred Jerome and

Jake Rosen of PL had spent months in Cuba following the Revolution and prior to the "travel ban". Upon their return to the U.S., they had tried to get the Cubans to subsidize a Cuban propaganda paper in this country to be run by the two of them. Jerome developed close relations with the Cuban Mission to the United Nations and was chosen by the PL leadership to organize the trip.

Following a Progressive Labor meeting in the fall of 1962 Jerome approached the Cubans with a suggested trip. The Cubans jumped at the opportunity and immediately appropriated half a million dollars. Progressive Labor then set up a group to coordinate a proposed trip for December 1962. Levi Laub, Steve Martinot, and Anatol Schlosser were chosen by PL to become the public leaders and spokesmen of the December trip. Jerome remained in the shadows.

Plans were completed in November, and the trip was scheduled for the Christmas holidays. The scheme included traveling to Canada and then flying to Cuba in a chartered Cuban plane. But when the group of nearly a hundred got to Canada, they discovered that the Canadians refused to allow the Cubans to land, and the December 1962 trip fell through.

Early in 1963, following this fiasco, Levi Laub was sent to Cuba to help the Cubans come up with some better travel arrangements. By the time Laub returned from Cuba with the final diagrams in his briefcase, more young people had agreed to join the trip. During this recruitment period, the role of Progressive Labor was continually played down, and few of the travelers knew that the trip was organized and fully controlled by PL, and even fewer knew of the role played by Fred Jerome. Everyone knew that some of the trip members were Communists and in Progressive Labor, but the "line" given to the travelers was not Communist. At the time we finally left for Havana via Paris and Prague, in the summer of 1963, we issued a press release that stated in part:

> We intend to break through the Cane-Curtain imposed by our State Department to limit travel to Cuba. A free, democratic society need have no fear from the truth. Our position parallels that of the *New York Post* editorial of September 19, 1957: "Somehow we

cannot escape the feeling that the government utterly lacks faith in the free play of democratic forces it so piously espouses. Freedom to travel cannot hurt a democracy."

After I wrote this press release, some of the more doctrinaire members of PL objected to my civil-libertarian style, but they were outvoted. The people who went to Cuba in the summer of 1963 were not merely tools of a PL operation. Most of them were independent leftists. It is doubtful whether anyone would have stayed home even if the full role of PL had been divulged. But ignorance of the underlying reasons for the trip and the identity of the real organizers allowed the majority of travelers to be used by PL for its own propaganda purposes. Fifty-nine people, who were later joined by eighty-four others, lost their passports, and some lost more, to feed the notoriety PL sought.

And we shook up the Cubans almost as much as we did the American State Department. The Cuba of 1963-64 was not the same as the post-Revolution Cuba of beards and berets. By that time the Revolution had been infiltrated by young bureaucrats with simpleminded Communist slogans and solutions. All of us went to Cuba with preconceived ideas, but our romantic image of the Cuban Revolution lagged after the first day in Havana.

During our European tour on the way to Havana we landed in Czechoslovakia. Czechoslovakia dented our romanticism. At one point on the 1963 trip, we almost called the whole thing off and came home because of the Czechs. When we arrived, the Czechs stuck us in the Hotel Moskva, located about fifty miles from Prague in the center of a health resort called Karlsbad. Karlsbad resembled the scenery in the movie *Last Year at Marienbad*, and the Communists in residence at the hotel represented bourgeois Communism at its worst. The hotel had its own little bar and dance floor, and every night the commissars gathered there with their women and danced the early evening away. The town itself closed up at about 9:30, and by 10 o'clock the streets had been rolled up. When we arrived in Karlsbad, our group was hardly the essence of revolutionary respectability. Beards and mustaches predominated, the girls wore Levis, and we also had a number of black people with us. None of this seemed to settle very well with the other residents of the hotel, and openly derisive remarks were made regarding the race of some of our travelers. Others simply made snide cracks about our dress and our manners. The attitudes of these bourgeois Communist soon became intolerable to us. Many of us had initially chosen the "left" because we felt that here appearances no longer mattered. The insults and discrimination we suffered in Karlsbad were very similar to what would have happened to us had we, as a group, entered the Waldorf-Astoria. We left the United States only to be confronted with a Communist bureaucracy as bigoted and "middle-class" as those we had left. The plane from Cuba arrived just in the nick of time, and we headed toward the forbidden land.

The scene at the Havana airport alone was worth the trip. Cuba still had enough Latin flavor in it to inspire the Revolution with a cha-cha beat. The hostility of the Czechs was matched by warm friendship from the Cubans. The drabness of the Czech state and the petit-bourgeois standards of the Prague Communists were set in contrast by the Cubans, who made us feel like conquering heroes. And there shining in the sun, overshadowing a portion of the airport, was a sign proclaiming Cuba "the free land of the hemisphere."

We took the Cubans rock-and-roll records, poetry books, and an outlook totally dissimilar from that of any other young people visiting Cuba from either the rest of Latin America or the world. The communist youth delegates from other countries stuck in my mind as the prototype of "concerned" revolutionaries. They were square and dull. With an abundance of crypto-theory in their minds, and with their eyes on the Cuban women, they discussed their importance in the "forthcoming revolutions" planned for their respective countries. We too had our eyes on the Cuban girls—who wouldn't?—but we were singularly untheoretical and undisciplined in both philosophical, political, and personal mannerisms. Our exuberance was applauded, while our behavior was considered strange.

(In some regards, the second group to go to Cuba was even

stranger. In June 1964, some of the delegates traveled to Paris on their journey via El Al, the Israeli airline. There was some thought that the government might try to stop the second trip, and the departure was arranged in secrecy, but when the delegates arrived at the airport it was obvious that secrecy was no problem. Most of the people booked on this flight were Orthodox Jews, and our people, replete with long beards and hair, melted into the group.)

Yes, there is no use denying the fact that we were the unkempt young people seen on TV and in the press. We were part of the bearded, mustached, blue-jeaned politicos that have been a part and parcel of almost every protest movement among young people in this country in the past few years.

Although the Cubans looked askance at us and our non-conformist ways, they tried to adjust to us. It of course helped that we looked as though we had just come out of the hills, a la Fidel in 1958.

Our independence even tried the patience of the Cuban bureaucrats. When we arrived, the Havana bureaucrats insisted on giving us the "guided tour" treatment. We refused this gesture immediately and won the right to have the majority of our time free to see what we wanted to see, when we wanted to. Throughout July and August 1963, we took long trips as a group. But in every city we had days on end when we simply wandered the streets by ourselves or with a member of the group who spoke Spanish. A surprisingly large number of the group did speak Spanish, so we were not constantly surrounded by government guides and had many candid conversations with the people.

While we were in Cuba, we saw the island and the government more freely than any other group of Americans that has visited there since the State Department "travel ban." Our conversations with Cuban government officials defy imagination. Can you conceive of a group of Russian or French Communists, or a group of American CP elders, cornering President Osvaldo Dorticos Torrado in his chambers and demanding to know why Cuba allowed the Russians to take out the missiles against the will of the Cuban people? We did it. And when we went to a cooperative farm in Rosario, in the heartland of Cuba, we asked an administrator of the farm why he had be appointed, instead of a farmer. When we learned that this administrator was merely appointed by the Cuban Farm Bureau because, according to him, he "could be trusted," we had a real session. The conversation went on for hours, and the administrator lost his temper, and so did we. The questions were neither polite nor appropriate for a visiting "fraternal" delegation.

We intended to stay in Cuba for only one month, but because of the impossible travel arrangements and our inability to fly the ninety miles to Florida directly, our trip eventually lasted two months. During that time, we toured the island from end to end, and because of our insistence on "free time" and unguided tours, we had the unique opportunity of meeting a vast cross section of the people. We naturally met with, and interviewed, the top leadership of the Cuban government. We played Ping-Pong with Fidel, discussed the farm development with Carlos Raphael Rodriguez, heard about the role of the Cuban Communist Party in the Revolution from Blas Roca, and had a candid question-and-answer period with Che Guevara.* We were

* I feel compelled to add this footnote in order that the reader might gain some insight into "Che" Guevara the now "sainted" apostle of the New Left.

We met Che in his office at the Department of Industries building. He looked just like his pictures—complete with the same intense stare and almost magnetic personality. No matter how you view it, Che was a real man and a devoted revolutionary. He spoke some English and was totally devoted to the cause of revolution. He slept in his office and ate the food of the peasants.

While we were with Che he told the following anecdote concerning himself and his then current job as head of Cuba's industries. According to Che, once the revolution was consummated and the power was in the hands of Fidel and company, a meeting was called. At this meeting it was decided to divide up the responsibilities. Fidel was the natural choice for premier as he was the acknowledged leader of the revolution. The next choice was Oswaldo Dorticos for President because he had been a lawyer and looked like a President.

From here on, the story line developed through the various governmental posts such as: Raul as the head of the army, Blas Roca as head of the press, Carlos Raphael Rodriguez as head of agriculture. Then they came to the question of who should control the economy and the industries. So, Che related that someone asked: "Who in here is an economist?" And, Che raised his hand. He was appointed head of the industries and the meeting went on. Later, in the hall, Raul walked up to Che and said: "Christ, Che, I didn't know that you were an economist." Che responded with: "Economist, my God, I thought they said 'Communist'."

This story is true and I can only rely on the reader to interpret it in his own manner.

constantly the center of some dialogue with governmental officials. We saw so many schools and talked with so many students that finally we called a halt to all attempts by the Cuban Student Federation (who paid for the trip) to place any more schools on our itinerary.

A few of us spent hours in private conversations with representatives of the Vietcong who were visiting Havana for the July 26th celebrations. I met the new leader of Algeria, Houari Boumedienne, before the vast majority of American diplomats even knew he existed. One evening I spent nearly two hours in a private conversation with the head of the Indonesian Communist Party, D. N. Aidit, who told me that the Indonesian Communists were contemptuous of the American Communist Party and were then only using the democratic process in Indonesia to the advantage of the Communists. He assured me, however, that as soon as it appeared as if the Communists were beginning to lose in the bid for power, they would institute a guerrilla war and topple the government. It is possible that I may be the only American to have discussed the possibility of an armed revolt in Indonesia with the man who was later to attempt just such an abortive move.

I met with a number of "counterrevolutionaries" who condemned the Castro regime and who wanted to leave Cuba and come to the United States. I spent hours talking with farmers who had just recently learned to read and write. One farmer was an outspoken supporter of the Revolution because for the first time in his life his children were now attending school. He spoke to me of the hardships and the limitations of the Communist Revolution, but he said that he overlooked much of the objectionable nature of the regime simply because now his children had the opportunity to get an education and to leave the farm and perhaps become doctors.

In a two-month period, you cannot become an expert on any country. All that you can expect, if you are diligent and not dependent on much sleep, is to capture a sense of the feeling of a small cross section of the population regarding their "new" government and their way of life. In Havana, I saw slums that were worse than those in Mississippi, in Santiago I saw new schools that were architecturally superior to most schools in this country, in the countryside I saw new farm communities with hospitals and schools serving people who had never previously seen the inside of a classroom and who had suffered for generations from various "peasant" diseases.

At the University of Santiago we asked how many students there had read *Flowers of Evil* by Baudelaire, and when only a few put up their hands, we were shocked and showed it. In Havana I met young artists and film makers who were experimenting and producing paintings, sculptures, and movies that flaunted the usual concept of "socialist realism." These young artists were as experimental and "new-wave" as most of their contemporaries in this country. I saw government-controlled whorehouses in Havana and stayed in a school city in the mountains that provided education for children who would never have learned to read or write prior to the Revolution.

Our two month stay in Cuba taught us that this country, like ours, is a land of contrasts. You could see new schools and hospitals. You could also see slums and poverty. At that juncture, the Cuban revolutionary spirit had begun to wane and the brutal reality of collectivism was becoming evident. You could see more schools but you also knew that the major push in education centered around Marxism-Leninism and the "proper" attitude towards both the state and revolution.

Throughout our tour we were plagued with the inner notion that we were receiving something better than the Cuban people. This came to a head one evening when we were out in the countryside being feted by a local revolutionary cadre. I was sitting at the head table with a military officer who had fought in the mountains with Fidel and as we ate our steaks he leaned over and said "Don't think that this is what we usually eat. You are getting the royal tour."

Still, those of us that went to Cuba expecting to find a near Nirvana returned with our rhetoric intact. I guess it will always be true that man sees what he wants to see. One young artist that we knew from earlier New York days had returned to Cuba because he felt that the millenium had arrived. He was a cousin to one of the revolutionary bureaucrats and he felt secure. He painted what he wanted and finally he got a free trip to China.

Peking, he told us, was a total drag. And the worst thing was the fact that you could not meet any Chinese girls. Finally, a letter arrived in New York from Communist China that told us that he had "clipped the wings of a low flying Chinese dove." Horrors! The Communists caught him and he was sent back to Cuba where he "worked out" his problem on a eucalyptus farm. When we got together in his apartment in Havana you had to doubt the efficacy of collectivism.

But the most tragic thing that happened during the 1963 trip was the death of my friend and comrade (in the real sense of the word) Hector Hill. Hector, a young Negro artist who was married and had three children, traveled with us, not because he was a Communist, but because he wanted to see what was happening to the children of Cuba. Hector wanted to draw their faces, their reactions, and their activities. He wanted to carry their essence back to his children in the U.S.A. and show them that Cuban children were really not much different from us. He felt lost, frustrated, and hated in white America, and after the social freedom he experienced while stationed in Europe, he thought that there had to be something better. He hoped it might be Cuba.

Prague and the Czechs weighed heavily on Hector, and he was thinking of giving the trip up, when we arrived in Havana. Once in Cuba, however, he began visiting artists, students, and young people. He spent hours just sitting and talking with them. We used to walk through the slums of Santiago and talk with the kids, watch them play in squalor, and think of Mississippi and Harlem. On the day that Hector drowned, he spent the morning away from the group, which had gone to inspect a steel mill or something, just talking with young children and sketching their portraits. He wanted to keep the sketches himself, but the kids wanted their own pictures so badly that he let them have them. That night we went to a huge carnival. Later, Hector went swimming in an unlit pool at the motel where we were staying and accidentally drowned. His death shocked each of us into his own private grief.

The Cubans did everything possible to help. The Swiss, representing the United States in Cuba, confirmed the death as an accidental drowning. Two of us met with Raul Roa, the

Cuban foreign minister, who attempted to ship the body back to New York and Hector's family. Roa agreed to allow a United States plane to land in Havana to take the body back or to fly it to New York in a Cuban Red Cross plane.

The American State Department rejected these plans. Instead, the only thing the United States would agree to was a landing of a Cuban Red Cross plane in Florida at a military base. This was done, but even then it wasn't over. The military refused to ship the casket to New York and for a time even refused to release it. Hector's family didn't have the money to send for the body, and it was left to Clark Foreman and Bill Worthy, the Negro journalist, to raise the needed money. We had persuaded Father Felix McGowan, a Catholic priest visiting Cuba, to accompany the casket, and it was only at his insistence that the military finally released it. And once the casket got to New York, the bureaucrats did their best to cause pain and delay. They refused to allow Hector's family to see the body or let the casket be opened for identification. They frustrated efforts to have a funeral, and they harassed his family.

This inhuman behavior on the part of various officials did more to turn the Cuban travelers against the United States government than anything we did or saw in Cuba. No matter what your political beliefs or your purported "crimes," you never expect your own country to be so callous.

Upon the return of the first group from Cuba in August of 1963, the travelers set up the Student Committee for Travel to Cuba (SCTC), controlled by an Executive Board composed of two PL members and three companions. (All had joined Progressive Labor by the time of the second trip in the summer of 1964.)

After our return from Cuba, the House Committee on Un-American Activities called us to Washington, where our rowdy outbursts in the hearing room led to a riot. The Federal government then indicted four of us for arranging the trip. Levi Laub, Steve Martinot, and I were all charged with going to and returning from Cuba, and along with Anatol Schlosser, were charged with "conspiring" to send others to Cuba. Schlosser did not make the trip, however, and broke with PL while we were there. Somehow the government missed Fred Jerome.

The SCTC spent the winter and spring of 1964 organizing another trip. This second trip did not attempt any subterfuge about the constitutional issues involved, but was strictly a political trip designed to embarrass the United States. It was then contended by the SCTC, now firmly under the control of Progressive Labor, that travel was a form of revolutionary activity. The magazine *Progressive Labor* contended that "travel to the 'forbidden lands' is useful to the development of a revolutionary ideology in the United States."

The second summer excursion to Cuba was in the worst of the James Bond tradition. The more bizarre aspects included the members of the SCTC filing false reservations at a number of airline offices to Bermuda and British Guiana to throw the government off as to how the trip was scheduled. The actual flight arrangements were then made by Mort Slater and Wendy Nakashima, through a travel agency. (Wendy Nakashima, Jake Rosen's wife, was associated with left-wing groups at CCNY and spent a month in Cuba in 1960.) The travel agent was so impressed with Mort and Wendy's efficiency that he not only bought the story of an art group going to Europe, but he actually offered Slater a job when he returned.

Our hide-and-seek activities culminated just a few days before the first of three groups left for Cuba. We suddenly discovered that a last-minute acceptance had told her father where she was going and he in turn had told the State Department and the FBI. The State Department held up her passport, and the Bureau paid her a visit. Since her apartment was unsafe for business transactions, we picked her up one evening on a street corner so we could see if anything could be arranged to get her out of the country. Immediately, another car pulled in behind us and began to follow. As we wove in and out of traffic, they stayed with us until a car that we had following them cut them off toward the curb. We escaped down a darkened street.

The Cubans managed to add their own theatrics by giving us the money for the last group of four travelers in an Alliance for Progress paper bag. This money came into the Cuban Mission at the UN in a diplomatic pouch.

We had chosen Ed Lemansky to lead the second trip. Lemansky, a graduate of Antioch College, was considered a conservative in his younger years, and many of his past associates have yet to understand his switch to Communism. Before the trip, Lemansky was in charge of the Progressive Labor operation in Monroe, North Carolina, where PL had tried to horn in on the apparatus Robert Williams surrendered when he escaped to Cuba.

Things went so well on the second trip that we kept pushing our luck and ended up sending three separate groups. All of them went the long route—Paris, Prague, and Havana. They came back the same way. Our second group was sent in an attempt to test the government's power to stop us. We called a press conference at the airport and watched the government agents look us over, but they did nothing to stop us. With this victory, we got cocky and sent another group of four. The travel plans were made in the open, another press conference was held, and the SCTC released a press statement that read in part:

> Today the Organization of American States (OAS) is meeting in Washington, D.C. Among the resolutions to be considered are those introduced by the American Government in its attempts to force the South American countries to cut off all ties with the Republic of Cuba . . . The Student Committee for Travel to Cuba proudly announces that it is sending four more young Americans to Cuba today to join the 80 other young Americans who have been visiting the island this summer.

Because the 1964 travelers returned through Prague and Paris, they missed out on Madrid. After two months in Cuba, most of the 1963 group had found Madrid an oasis of relief. And although some of the zealots, led by the young Stalinist Steve Martinot, refused to spend any money in the "fascist" country, the rest of us painted Madrid "red" while they sat in the hotel. The Cubans, by the way, unintentionally paid for our Madrid party with money they had given us to bring back to the United States.

Nine indictments were handed down following the 1964 trip. After thirteen of the travelers were indicted, some on multiple counts that might result in possible jail terms of up to 20 years, the leadership of PL decided against further trips. They dropped the public-relations campaign against the travel ban, and their support of those indicted. While the issue of free travel became a widely discussed issue in the press and on college campuses, the leaders of PL dropped the cause for bigger and better things.

Fred Jerome appeared at a special meeting of the governing board of the SCTC in December and told us that he thought "we have gotten all the mileage out of the travel issue that we can." Over some strenuous opposition, the proposed trip for the summer of 1965 was shelved. Youth activities were diverted toward actions protesting the war in Vietnam.

Ultimately, a trial did take place. My case was "severed" from that of Laub, Martinot and Schlosser. The government wanted me to plead "guilty" and testify against my fellow indictees. I refused, but I did testify at the trial regarding the actual plans made to travel to Cuba and the role Progressive Labor had in those plans. However, I believed then as I believe now, in the inherent right of an American citizen to travel where he wants to travel when he wants to travel.

The federal court agreed with our contention that the State Department did not have the legal power to tell American citizens what countries they might visit and the Supreme Court refused to consider the government's appeal.

THE RISE OF
PROGRESSIVE LABOR

5

BY the end of 1961, the Communist Party of the U.S.A. had decayed too much to be rejuvenated. The Federal government, acting through its legislative branch, had already saddled the Party with the blight of oppressive control laws. The Smith Act had sent a number of leading Communists to jail for "advocating the violent overthrow of the government." The McCarran Act was now doing its best to ensure that the CPUSA "registered" its members, assets, and printing equipment with the government. These laws, along with the Cold War, turned the CPUSA into a defense organization—a defense organization whose prime purpose was to defend itself against further encroachments upon its dwindling membership.

The small meetings held in New York City, the center of CP activity in the country, in 1961 and 1962 centered on this defense effort. Although the courts had not definitively decided the status of the McCarran Act, and therefore neither the Party nor its members had to "register" as prescribed by law, the court battles bled the party of funds and militants needed to achieve an aggressive stance.

Flagging membership and loss of funds are not the only reasons for the lackluster appearance of the CPUSA. The Party also has a responsibility as the non-registered agent of the Soviet Union, and in the era of peaceful co-existence, it wouldn't do to have the CPUSA running around openly advocating the violent overthrow of the American government. How would the comrades in Moscow explain this to the American State Department? The CPUSA members therefore play the devious role of trying to pass as "socialist" moderates. While keeping its contacts with the Soviet espionage apparatus, the CPUSA openly advocates only acts designed to sow confusion and chaos throughout the political spectrum. But by advocating a moderate revolutionary course, the CPUSA has paid the penalty of isolating itself from the growing population of aroused student leftists.

The CPUSA represents the peaceful-coexistence views of the Kremlin and is composed largely of around 12,000 oldsters. Many of these oldsters are little old ladies whose actions are more of a menace to themselves than to the country.

The Progressive Labor group stole the spotlight from the CPUSA. It pulled the spotlight toward itself with an approach that fluctuated between a flair for the preposterous and an understanding of the political tenor of the young Communist mind.

By 1961 "left-wing" elements in the CPUSA had made their move to try to "radicalize" the Party. This "left wing" within the CPUSA was led by Milt Rosen and Mort Scheer. Rosen, who is over forty, six feet in height, and developing a paunch, was the New York state labor chieftain of the CP. Scheer, who is the same age, was the CPUSA organizer in Buffalo, New York, where his college degree had gotten him a job as an elevator operator. Both of these men had run for the National Committee of the CPUSA in 1959, and following their defeat had formed a faction envisioned as identical to the "Albanian line." Albania, at that time, was the chief whipping post for the Soviet Union and the lone pilgrim in the field favoring Peking.

Rosen and Scheer, along with a few other disgruntled "comrades," began actively to suggest the CPUSA move its headquarters to Chicago, change its name and image, and if necessary "go underground" to bypass the many anti-Communist laws that exist. Perhaps then, they argued, the CPUSA might again take the offensive. *Militancy über alles.*

It appears that Rosen, Scheer, and their followers had some weight in the Party, because George Morris, writing in the Communist Party weekly reader, *The Worker,* claims these two renegades had actually lined up some pigeons before they were booted out. Morris wrote that the "views of Rosen were espoused in the Negro-American Labor Council of Buffalo and New York where they temporarily held some key posts."

But the Negro-American Labor Council is not the CPUSA. So in October of 1961, the CPUSA sent Ben Davis, then known as a "spokesman" for the Party, now deceased, to Buffalo to straighten out Scheer and his cronies. When Scheer refused to knuckle under to the edicts of the CP oligarchy, he was duly expelled. Rosen met a similar fate in the Party headquarters in New York City.

This created a problem for both Rosen and Scheer. Since neither man was equipped to do much more than organize for the Communists, they decided to try to cash in on the crisis in the international movement and to side with the Chinese.

They decided to start their own Communist Party and challenge the CPUSA over who would "lead the revolution." The first act of these few orphans of Communism was to set up a magazine to express their views. The founding of the periodical *Progressive Labor* by Rosen and Scheer gave them a vehicle upon which to begin the crusade for the Chinese political line.

The split in the international Communist world increased in those months, and suddenly Rosen and Scheer found that they had splinter comrades in many of the Western countries. In Belgium and New Zealand, the Chinese sympathizers were able to wrest control of the existing parties. In England, France, Italy, Australia, Canada, and the United States, new organizations were formed to challenge the "revisionist" leadership of the Moscow-controlled CPs. In England the Maoist group went under the unwieldy title of the Committee to Defeat Revisionism for Communist Unity, while in Canada it became the Progressive Workers Party. In France, the Chinese advocates joined behind a publication aptly entitled *Revolution*. Revolution, with a plush, six-color cover, attracted Chinese advocates from all over the world. The Soviet Union took offense at its "Madison Avenue format" and rightly deemed it a tool of the Chinese warmongers.

Here in the United States, Progressive Labor simply jumped from the cover of a publication to the title of an organization. Scheer and Rosen immediately began trying to pull together a cohesive body of people who could effectively fight the CPUSA and create a "new" body of Communism. The bandied-about theory that Progressive Labor was formed by the CPUSA in an attempt to take the legal pressures off by creating a radical "front" is incorrect. The views of those expelled from the CPUSA (about twenty-five at that time) were out of context with the prevailing views of the hierarchy. Absolutely no love existed between the New Communists and the "old-liners."

Progressive Labor lost little time in declaring the CPUSA "a hopeless apologist for imperialism." The CPUSA responded to this broadside with aplomb, and Gus Hall, General Secretary of the CP, labeled PL as "parasitic on the Chinese position just as they are parasites on the civil-rights movement." This spirit of "fraternity" has not diminished. At the founding of Progressive Labor in April of 1965, Milt Rosen noted how the Old Communists of "the CPUSA capitulated, leaving the path clear for the ruling class ideology." The CP has responded in kind with various editorials denouncing these usurpers from the East. The members of Progressive Labor might well be identified as the "White Chinese." They jokingly call their organization "the friends of Guozi Shudian," in honor of the Peking distributor of Communist propaganda.

Since its 1961 baptism, Progressive Labor has remained the formal name of the organization. This title was not, however, as original as its new adherents would have you believe. The name was actually borrowed from a group, organized in the 1930s under the tutelage of A. J. Muste, which billed itself as the conference for Progressive Labor Action. This defunct PL was responsible for the early political education of such American Communist Party functionaries as Arnold Johnson, CPUSA public relations man. Dr. Muste renounced the Communist path and came to be recognized as the grand old man of the American pacifist movement. He had no dealings with the new PL organization.

The last serious attempt to change the name of Progressive Labor to something a bit more sexy came prior to the April 1965 convention. An attempt was made at that time to jazz up the namesake by rebaptizing the PLP as the American Revolutionary Movement (ARM) and its youth section as the American Revolutionary Movement Youth (ARMY). This proposal was defeated with straight faces.

Within the first year of activity, Progressive Labor drew in all of what has since come to be known as the "leadership." Milt Rosen graciously accepted the post of chairman of the Progressive Labor Party. Mort Scheer, who then headed the San Francisco PL operation, was given the office of one of the vice-chairmen. The other vice-chairman, who doubled as the Harlem chairman of PL, was Bill Epton. Epton, a former CPUSA electrician, is best known for his role in the Harlem riots of the summer of 1964. Epton was indicted for "criminal anarchy," or attempting to overthrow the state government, and was later convicted. Then in 1970, Epton was suddenly "expelled" from PL.

The CPUSA also gave two of its more militant youth leaders, Jake Rosen and Fred Jerome, to the Progressive Labor founders. These two were also expelled from the CP on charges similar to those lodged against Milt Rosen, Scheer, and their group. When Jerome and Jake Rosen joined PL, they brought with them a background in Communist operations among young people, youthful impatience, vitality, and a hard-bitten practical approach to organization.

Fred Jerome, a thin, bookish sort, suffered from extreme nervousness and an ulcer. A graduate of City College in New York, he edited a school newspaper. Later, he gained a background in magazine layout while working for *Newsweek*. His father, V. J. Jerome, was formerly the editor of *Political Affairs,* the CPUSA's theoretical organ, and remained a member of the CPUSA until his death in August of 1965. Fred Jerome was given his father's assumed name of "Jerome." V. J. Jerome was in reality Jerome Isaac Romain, and it is jokingly rumored that the initials "V. J." stood for J. V. (Stalin) spelled backwards.

As a CP organizer, Jerome helped found Advance, the New York CP youth organization, a fact he refused to admit during a Congressional investigation. He spent nine months in Cuba in 1960 and lived under an alias in Atlanta, Georgia, after his return to this country. When Che Guevara came to the United Nations in January of 1965, Jerome and Levi Laub held a secret conference with him at the Cuban Mission to the UN. Jerome, as a member of the National Committee of PL, was moved from the editorship of the PL weekly newspaper, *Challenge*, to the editorship of their monthly journal, *Progressive Labor*. His brother, Carl, was active as a PL organizer on the Lower East Side of New York until he apparently went "underground" and dropped out of sight. Following the birth of his son, Fred Jerome followed suit and also dropped from public sight. He was gone for about six months, and was not again seen in New York until January 1966.

Jake Rosen, who is the same age as Jerome, is not related to Milt Rosen. He sometimes doubles as the alter ego to Jerome's humorless temperament. Robust and overtly aggressive, Rosen is given to a flashing smile and a strong handshake. He tries to "sell" Communism like a used-car salesman. A graduate of City College of New York, Rosen is "married" to Wendy Nakashima, a Progressive Labor recruit from the CP.* He was an organizer of the American delegation to the Moscow World Youth Festival in 1957, and then led a side excursion to China. While he was in China, Rosen made headlines in the daily newspaper

---

*Within the existing Progressive Labor mind, at that moment in history, the decision was made to pair off certain people in "marriages." The PLP functionaries held meetings to decide who would bed with whom, and who would be unbedded. At one of these meetings we decided that a particular young woman, whose father was a wealthy literary critic, should be "studded" by one of our more youthful members. At another juncture, we decided that the relationship between my former wife and her comrade had to be destroyed because we thought he might be a spy. I was therefore delegated the job of breaking them up and taking her over.

of CCNY, *The Campus*. The lead story of October 16, 1957, announced that Jake Rosen was unflatteringly "found hanged in effigy on the North Campus yesterday. A four-foot-high dummy representing Rosen was discovered by passing students early yesterday morning. It was dangling from the post of a traffic light across the street from Lewisohn Stadium at 138th Street. Rosen is not expected to return to the college until next semester."

In 1960, Jake Rosen went to Cuba and worked with an "international youth brigade." Upon his return he was put in charge of various goon squads that patrolled the Fair Play for Cuba Committee meetings in New York City. These goon squads were strong, hefty young men who would patrol the meeting and "bounce" any who might try to be disruptive of the proceedings. Their treatment was none too gentle.

Rosen has been a Communist ever since his childhood days at the CPUSA's summer camps located in upstate New York. According to sworn testimony before a Congressional committee, Rosen denounced an American newsman, Charles Wiley, to the Cuban secret police as an "anti-Communist." Mr. Wiley spent eight days in a Cuban jail as a result.

Rosen also played a key role, often that of a factionalist, trying to get power by controlling splinter groups, in the Advance organization, until his expulsion from the CPUSA. During the summer of 1961, he lived in Augusta, Georgia, under the alias of John Harnett.

Since joining Progressive Labor, Jake Rosen has worn a number of hats. He has been a member of the National Committee and was in charge of the Party convention in April of 1965. Prior to this, he was the editor of the PL southern newspaper *Freedom* and the "southern editor" of *Progressive Labor*. Rosen was perhaps best known, however, as a "traveler." At various times during the year, Jake Rosen would simply "disappear" for a period of time and then suddenly turn up again. Members of the organization were led to believe that he went "south" on these sojourns, but no one in the organization saw him there.

As a result of the April 1965 convention, the Progressive Labor Party came up with a formal organization and a Party

Constitution. The framework of the PL organization is almost an exact carbon copy of the CP organization. A re-reading of the 1938 "Constitution and By-Laws" of the CPUSA shows the remarkable similarity that exists between the two groups. In 1938 Old Communists put it this way: "The National Committee is the highest authority of the Party." The New Communists, showing a disregard for originality of thought, stated "The National Convention shall elect the National Committee which shall be responsible, as the highest body of the Party between conventions, to give leadership to the Party and to carry through all policies of the Convention." PL's statement distinguishes itself only by its excessive verbosity.

At the April 1965 convention a twenty-man National Committee was elected from a slate of thirty-two candidates. Five of the candidates on the ballot were disguised and were only identifiable from descriptions of their PL work. Rosen was crowned chairman at this convention. A few other National Committee members are worth noting for their influence in PL.

Levi Laub's election to the National Committee was an obvious choice. Laub is a tall, articulate, fraternity type. His wealth was obtained from his marriage to Mary Maher, the daughter of a Texas millionaire, who was one of the people who went to Cuba in the summer of 1964. Laub himself was the acknowledged leader of the 1963 trip to Cuba, which earned him a Federal indictment upon his return.

Laub, a former Columbia University student, was the only member of the "top" leadership who was not trained in the CPUSA prior to joining Progressive Labor. Although Laub was one of the most impressive in the organization and exhibited at one time an independence from the Communist conformity, he too took on the trappings of total thought control. Originally considered an opportunist by many in and out of PL, Laub gradually dropped his individualistic approach to Communism as he climbed toward leadership. He sank to impromptu lectures on "democratic centralism" and other Communist double-talk concepts. Subsequently, Laub also served a jail sentence in a New York state prison for contempt of a New York grand jury.

One of the lesser-known personalities around progressive Labor was Sue Warren, who wrote the weekly column for *Challenge* on world affairs under the pseudonym of Lisa Armand, a name presumably adapted from Lenin's mistress—Inessa Armand. At the April 1965 convention Mrs. Warren was disguised on the ballot as a "leader in ideological work." She was one of the few women on the National Committee and was formerly one of the "China experts" for the CPUSA. She traveled extensively throughout China and developed numerous contacts on the mainland. She also traveled to Algeria for the abortive Afro-Asian Conference planned for June of 1965. In Progressive Labor circles, Sue Warren was considered an expert on Chinese affairs, although most of her present knowledge came from the daily Hsinhua (New China News Agency) reports sent to PL from London. The New China News Agency has an office in London in exchange for the right of a British news service to operate in China.

Walter Linder was also elected to the National Committee. Linder is a veteran Communist who was sent by the Party, fresh from graduate school with an M.A. in history, into the factories as part of their "industrial concentration" program. Members designated for "industrial concentration" work were supposed to be the organizing force for a big Communist drive to take over some basic industries, such as steel. Another purpose was to take some bourgeois elements in the CPUSA and give them direct contact with "the working class." The hope was that they would discover the beauty of the life of a worker and thereby lose their more bourgeois concepts. On both accounts, the program was a failure, although it ended the futures of a number of bright young college graduates. Some had wasted as many as ten to fifteen years in these factory programs and couldn't get other jobs when they wanted to leave. They got stuck in this "concentration" and were never able to escape the factory or their CP membership, even after they realized their mistake and the CP abandoned this harebrained scheme.

In theory, the National Committee is the top leadership in Progressive Labor. Also in theory, it is responsible and responsive to the body of PL members. In reality, however, the "Party" is run on the principle of "democratic centralism," which is simply the principle of totalitarianism. The "top dogs" of Progressive Labor make the decisions for the organization, and the membership is directed to carry out orders.

The elite leaders were Milt Rosen, Mort Scheer, Jake Rosen, and Fred Jerome. There were a few "near-elite" people such as Epton and Laub, but everyone else was strictly second string.

The leaders also lived up to their titles. Just as the CPUSA "leader," Gus Hall, shows his ironic concern for the "working class" he so idolizes by living in a huge home in suburban Westchester County, N.Y., and arranges to be chauffeured to work every day, so do the PL leaders live well. They have copied another page from the Old Communists. Milt Rosen, as biggest "leader," lives the best. And interestingly enough, although his weekly paycheck from PL was in 1965 about $50, he was able to raise three children and support a nonworking wife in a sprawling apartment in Brooklyn. Rosen's low "salary" does not hinder him from owning a car or vacationing at a summer cottage on the ocean. A closely guarded secret is that, although apparently healthy, Rosen actually suffers from a heart condition. He is chauffeured around on occasion because of the Party's fear that he might get into a fight, for Rosen did have a history of fistfights with "reactionaries" in demonstrations and union struggles.

Some of the other comrades live as well. Rosen, Jerome, and Scheer all live in a similar manner, far beyond what their public salaries enable them to do. The subsidy that supports their accelerated standard of living comes from unidentified sources.

Others have less trouble balancing family budgets. Levi Laub, for instance, has insured himself against winter's cold by his wife's wealth. Albert Maher, Mary Maher Laub's brother, put up the $10,000 bail for Bill Epton when he was indicted for criminal anarchy. Albert Maher is himself under indictment for his role in organizing the second Cuban trip in the summer of 1964. Maher was enrolled in 1964–1965 at Harvard, where he headed the Harvard Progressive Labor group and the PL "front" for students, the May Second Movement. He was also nominated for the National Committee of PL in April 1965.

Actually, Progressive Labor might well afford to pay their leadership more money and cut out the under-the-table dealings. Although Progressive Labor publicly dresses as the

CPUSA's country cousin, there is evidence pointing to a rich uncle. Staff salaries on the PL newspaper *Challenge* ranged from $45 a week to $95 in the summer of 1965. The only person receiving as much as $95 was the feature writer Selma Sparks. Selma Sparks, one of the least dedicated fellow travelers, took the job on *Challenge* as a business proposition. Formerly a writer for the *Liberator*, a black revolutionist magazine, Mrs. Sparks earned a substantial salary increase when she joined the *Challenge* staff.

The membership of Progressive Labor represents strands of American society as apparently unrelated as the sons and daughters of Old Communists and the siblings of at least one millionaire. There are left-wing Black Muslims and at least one White Muslim. High school dropouts rub shoulders with pre-medical students and graduate students. Poets and folk singers outcant each other in revolutionary fervor. Most of this membership is under twenty-five, militant, and lacks any formal Marxist training, with the exception of those recruited from the CP.

Until the lid was clamped down in 1965, Progressive Labor was noted for its freewheeling approach to problems and activities. Discipline that was used to create conformity in dress and the espousal of political ideas was negligible, and, although Rosen and his court held sway over the whole scene, there was a considerable amount of individual initiative. But the youthful approach of the membership often collided with the "rejuvenated Communism" of the leadership. The young members were interested in action and had little use for theory. A little bit of Marx, Mao, and Milt Rosen, topped with Norman Mailer, made for radical speeches and proposals.

Prior to the edicts regarding dress, hair cutting, and beard shaving, the comrades from China would have been quite dismayed with the average member of Progressive Labor. PL became publicly identified with young men in Buffalo Bill mustaches, cowboy boots, and Levi pants. And, in the beginning, this romantic image surrounding Progressive Labor did the selling job for getting new recruits. While the leadership was Old Communist in morals, manners, and social patterns, the membership represented the New Left outlook. The old Communists represented those interested in accepted dress, in marriage, in frowning on the smoking of pot or the taking of LSD and mescaline. The initial appeal of PL also stemmed from its frankness in admitting it was a Communist organization and exposing its ties to the Chinese and the Cubans, and its apparent willingness to accept the "Beat Politicos."

Jack Newfield, writing in the *Village Voice,* typified the attitude of the democratic left toward the PL members before the crackdown in April 1965. He wrote that "Today's typical communist is young, candid, bohemian, violent, witty, pragmatic and identifies with the Cuban revolution. He reads anything from Swift to LeRoi Jones and listens to anything from Cuban folk melodies to John Coltrane. And he belongs to the Progressive Labor Movement."

Unfortunately, stereotyping Progressive Labor at any period does not tell the full story. The Old Communists still ran the show, and the young rebels who joined PL were rapidly being taught not to dissent within ranks. The creation of a "romantic" image helped to draw the young, alienated radical into the Progressive Labor orbit, but it was misleading.

While there were still some young people in Progressive Labor who listened to rock, read Swift, smoked pot, and socialized, this type of member rapidly became extinct. Pressures from the top to clean up the image of the organization, coupled with the demanding schedule of a full-time Communist, allowed little time for personal pleasures. According to the records of the Party convention in April 1965, the members were called upon to "defeat bourgeois ideology in our midst." Milt Rosen went on to declare that "we must rid ourselves also of idealism." From now on, according to Rosen, "we are undertaking not a game, not some fun, not something interesting, not something romantic, but undertaking to defeat the strongest imperialist power that has ever existed."

It is becoming increasingly difficult for Progressive Labor to be as aggressive as the Chinese Communists, but they took a step in showing their critics where they stood. They opened a Chinese bookstore, on Fifth Avenue in New York City, called "China Publications." It was run by David Rosen, the father of

Jake Rosen. If there was still any doubt who controlled this operation, David Rosen cleared it up when he "registered," in compliance with the provisions of the Foreign Agents Registration Act, with the United States government as an "agent" of the Chinese Communists.

When the burgeoning New Left was still in its state of rebellion against society *per se*, and its focal points centered in the writings and utterances of Mills, Sartre, Ginsberg, Trocchi, Norman Mailer, and James Baldwin, its essence was a lack of organization in its approach to change. But when the young rebel broke with the freewheeling atmosphere of the New Left and joined the New Communists surrounding Progressive Labor, he suddenly found himself in the camp of the revolutionaries.

Progressive Labor, in its Constitution adopted in April 1965, states that members "resolve to build a revolutionary movement" and "to build a socialist USA, with all power in the hands of the working people and their allies." To this end, the Progressive Labor Communists vowed their "lives" according to the Constitution.

Milt Rosen is not the Zen master, the reincarnation of Lenin, that he pretends he is, but a close-minded Communist interested in creating and abetting armed insurrection in this country. For all of his amiability and public stance of "Who, me?", Rosen has privately made it clear what he wants. At a secret meeting of the National Coordinating Committee of PL held in October 1964, Rosen stated: "In that sense we have to be very clear what we mean by revolutionary, and I want to underline Morty's [Scheer] point of view, because when I talk about revolutionary what I mean is that you want to overthrow the system and have the dictatorship of the proletariat."

For a time, Milt Rosen conducted classes for new initiates in Progressive Labor dealing with the correct Marxist-Leninist attitude regarding revolution. The text he used in these courses was *State and Revolution* by V. I. Lenin, and it was these two quotations that were stressed: (1) "We have already said above and shall show more fully later that the teaching of Marx and Engels regarding the inevitability of a violent revolution refers to the bourgeois state. It *cannot* be replaced by the proletarian state (the dictatorship of the proletariat) through 'withering

away,' but, as a general rule, only through a violent revolution."
(2) "The replacement of the bourgeois by the proletariat state is impossible without a violent revolution."

The top leadership of Progressive Labor decided in the spring of 1964 that rebels still had too much freedom in the organization. The Old Communists were becoming more and more concerned with the cavalier attitude of the membership, and new rules were imposed to force them into a more rigid mold. Every member of Progressive Labor must belong to a club and attend its weekly meetings, he must be a part of a weekly study group, he must sell the newspaper two hours a week, he must engage in "grass roots work among the masses" (a phrase stolen from some of the worst writings of the 1930s), he must buy all the Party literature, pay dues, and contribute to a sustaining fund as well.

This is all designed to force the membership into complete identification with the Party. Private lives are also being regulated, and we now witness "party marriages" similar to those practiced by the CPUSA in the 1930s, when the edict went out that all those who were living together had to get married.

Controls are getting tighter and tighter in the organization, so that good Communists and revolutionaries will be created. What those rebels left in PL don't understand is that the type of revolution that Rosen and his camp followers want would curb their individual freedom and activities. In fact, the first people to be purged, once the PL Communists "took power," would be iconoclasts. The rebellious nature of much of the PL membership would not be tolerated under a revolutionary socialist regime, and they would soon suffer the fate of the rebels in Russia and China. Milt Rosen's idol, Joe Stalin, clearly paved the way for the purges. The individualism of the young rebel in Progressive Labor is a life force the Communist zealots cannot allow to exist for very long.

In 1965 and 1966, the "White Chinese" leadership began to insist that art be an arm of politics. The poetry and graphics appearing in any PL publication are all political in nature. Although the New Communists are not particularly sensitive to combining the language of the streets or four-letter words with political poems about love, they were not about to allow too much artistic license. For example, the lead contribution to the May—June 1965 issue of *Progressive Labor* was a "poem" by Les Turner entitled "How to Be a Good Communist."

Although Progressive Labor has made some impact on some student intellectuals, they have not sucked very many into their mental quicksand.

Bob Dylan, one of America's best-known folk singers, while somewhat taken with PL's outrageously audacious manner, has repeatedly put them down for their totalitarianism and for their simpleminded and close-minded approach to problems. Joan Baez, another faithful of the young rebels, who has taken strong political stands against the war in Vietnam and has refused to pay taxes for armaments, has also had nothing to do with PL. I have heard her become outraged with the PL line and their support for the use of violence. Writing in Paul Krassner's *Realist*, Larry Cole, a professional social worker, has taken the Progressive Labor fanatics to task. Cole shot the PL heavies down when he wrote that:

> "Progressive", "Labor" and "Movement" as used in the PLM are as much a part of double-think vocabulary as the "clean bomb." "Progressive" and "Labor" have no meaning in the PLM scheme of things. Their method is reaction. They are certainly not a working class body. "Movement" implies solidarity.
>
> On the front of the PLM "Integrated Workers Club" on East 3rd Street is a sign in Spanish and English. It tells the local citizenry that between the hours of 8 and 10 on Tuesday nights the organization takes complaints about housing, police brutality, injustice in the courts and school. Two hours a week in a neighborhood where these problems are the rule, not the exception, would appear to be somewhat less than adequate. I see this as a hook to recruit shock troops. In PLM's chess game, they are expendable pawns.

Of course, no one should think that everyone in Progressive Labor is being duped by Svengali Rosen. The membership of Progressive Labor generally considers itself Communist. The idols are Mao, Fidel, and Kim Il Sung. A sign in a New York subway contained a slogan that may be a symbolic sign for the future. Emblazoned in bright-red letters were the words, "Mao,

Malcom X, Milt Rosen." Marx was lost in the alphabet soup.

All too many of the PL adherents have no sense of history and the real nature of Communism. The leadership calls for revolution, but gives no program for its achievement, and the membership has only a vague, romantic concept of revolution. The young members want a change in the political and social structure of the United States and have bought the sleazy slogan of "socialist revolution" as the cure-all. Some of the young people surrounding PL actually envision some kind of gargantuan revolution sweeping the United States, with Milt Rosen on a black charger clearing the path. Their own delusions and wish fulfillments are coupled with an avid reading of James Bond.

But the leadership knows what it is doing. Although it has not fully outlined its program for revolution, it knows the strategy to use to foment and spread attempts at armed revolt. This is not kid's play. It involves the use of arms and instruction in how to make bombs and utilize them.

The non-Communist left is especially reticent to expose the unlawful antics of PL for fear of being thought anti-civil-libertarian. Of course PL does its own bit to confuse the issue by claiming that it is being illegally prosecuted and persecuted at every bend in the road to revolution. No one would deny the "White Chinese" the right to all of the provisions and guarantees of the Constitution except when they involve themselves in illegal activities. The non-Communist left also has a responsibility to expose the Stalinist tendencies and illegal activities of Progressive Labor. Only when the rebels on the non-Communist left discover that their own programs and method for dissent are incompatible with those of the New Communists will they make a major break-through toward providing answers to the problems of their society.

The democratic left, as a whole, with some exceptions, contents itself with broadsides against the ultra-right lunatic fringe, and lacks both the energy and the political integrity to disinfect its own political camp.

The Communists count on a receptive hearing in the leftist student body. While they may pose as "constitutional" Communists, only demanding a right to be heard, the record of

Progressive Labor shows that they are intending to use any and every means to create a state of anarchy in this country. Exposure, constant discussion, and refutation of their doctrines and methods is necessary if young people are to avoid the trap of Communism. Most of the Communist claims of having "instant answers to all your problems" readily dissolve when mixed with informed criticism.

DECLINE AND FALL FOR PROGRESSIVE LABOR

THE fact that Progressive Labor is a Communist organization frequently following the dictates of the Chinese Communist Party does not, by itself, qualify it as a potential danger to our government. The rigors of membership in the Progressive Labor Party and its Stalinist tendencies only create a mental brick wall for the members of this sect. The Progressive Labor Party and its vacuum-minded Communists should not be marked for governmental control merely because they are Communist. The illegal actions of PL do, however, make it abruptly clear that this organization is deeply involved in plans and programs inimical to both our government and the concept of democracy, and they should be carefully watched.

A few die-hards argue that the Progressive Labor Party is no menace to democracy. They complain that because Progressive Labor has only a negligible mass base and is an "open" Communist apparatus, it is being harassed and persecuted by the power structure. These well-intentioned people contend that as a result of the "McCarthy hysteria," the Communists have been painted as much worse than they really are.

In some cases this is true. And coupled with the impact of subsequent, overstated verbal broadsides, the Communists are often credited with having cornered the "Mr. Hyde" market. But such a devil theory of Communism adds little to any rational discussion of the beast. The record of Progressive Labor's adventures in the revolutionary arena brand it far better than any devil theory.

In the ten years of its existence, Progressive Labor has found itself the focal point for numerous revolutionary acts. Its role in the Harlem riots in the summer of 1964, its two illegal student trips to Cuba, its attempt to move "underground," and its formation of a student group actively "toying with sedition," has shown the PLP as an organization worthy of some kind of governmental control.

This is not a group of young people simply flaunting their alienation from society and parents. This is a cult of 'true believers.' The PLP is a Communist party in the United States devoted to trying, through deceit, force, and violence, to gain power. Progressive Labor is dangerous to our democracy and especially dangerous to its own members who have little idea of the hidden objectives of the leaders whom they follow. The Progressive Labor Party has already created its niche in the annals of the American lunatic fringe. Progressive Labor constitutes a menace for the young person looking for radical solutions to today's political plights.

There is no doubt that Progressive Labor makes out its own best case against itself. Undoubtedly, one of its most important contributions to the "revolution" was its role in the riots that swept Harlem in the summer of 1964.

Of course Progressive Labor did not start the Harlem riots—either through its proclaimed revolutionary zeal or its alleged radicalization of Harlem residents. PL did, however, sieze upon an incident involving police and a young Harlem black, and used this incident to spur hard-core radical elements to action.

Lt. Thomas Gilligan, an off-duty police officer, witnessed a dispute involving a building superintendent and a Harlem youth who claimed the superintendent, while cleaning the building's sidewalk area, intentionally turned a hose on him. Lt. Gilligan approached the two, displayed his badge and inquired about the problem. The boy pulled a knife and attacked Gilligan. Gilligan, defending himself, drew his revolver and shot the boy. This was the spark that blew the summer wide open.

But, even as the Communist Party concluded in a *Worker* article on November 15, 1964, Progressive Labor did play a "provocative role in the recent Harlem riots."

On July 18, Bill Epton spoke to an open-air rally in Harlem, and in a crescendo of revolutionary fervor shouted, "We will not be fully free until we smash this state completely and totally. Destroy and set up a new state of our own choosing and our own liking . . . and in the process of smashing this state we're going to have to kill a lot of these cops, a lot of these judges, and we'll have to go up against their army. We'll organize our own militia and our own army." One hour later, the riots began.

That Saturday night and during the bloody week that followed, Progressive Labor was in the full swing of things. Epton and Bill McAdoo, who were heading the Harlem Defense Council, a PL "front," had almost hourly meetings with rioters. Discussions took place in the Progressive Labor office in Harlem concerning the making of molotov cocktails and incendiary bombs. Thousands of now famous "Wanted for Murder—Gilligan the Cop" posters were printed in the PL printshop. These posters were distributed throughout Harlem by the members of PL, and during the week of the riots the PL newspaper *Challenge* ran headlines screaming "Police Terror."

At the "criminal anarchy" trial of Epton, a police "undercover" detective introduced taped conversations that Epton held with various Harlem revolutionaries in which he discussed the use of molotov cocktails and continued resistance to police pacification of the riot area.

The lead editorial in *Challenge* during the week of the riots stated that "the rebellion . . . will not end soon—in fact, indications are that it is spreading throughout the City. The vision of half a million—or a million—angry black men and women, supported by allies in the Puerto Rican and other working class communities, standing up to their oppression, is haunting the ruling class. People have already begun to speak of 'guerrilla warfare' and 'revolutionaries.' " This editorial went on to urge the people not to "stay home from the freedom fight."

But one of the most outrageous acts of Progressive Labor during the riots took place on August 1, 1964, when Fred Jerome, the editor of *Challenge* at this juncture, signed an editorial advocating open anarchy. Jerome said, "I urge and will continue to urge and attempt to induce and persuade public demonstration in the streets of Harlem . . . I advocate precisely that the people disturb the peace . . . Let us not run and let us not pray—let us fight back . . . There is no lawful government in this country today. Only a revolution will establish one. If that is civil rebellion, let us make the most of it."

While Harlem was erupting, the PL club on the Lower East Side of New York City considered a riot of its own as a diversionary maneuver to pull the police out of Harlem. This is fully documented in the secret report of the PL National Coordinating Committee of October 1964.

Bill Epton complained that "we didn't get the support we needed and could have gotten from the East Side Club." Alice Jerome, head of the Lower East Side Club, and the mother of Fred Jerome, jumped into the discussion at this point and explained that "there was a time when we could have gone along with and participated in and helped to stimulate a much more widespread uprising on the Lower East Side, as part of our expression of support and solidarity with what was going on in Harlem, and we very consciously didn't do it. We tried to evaluate our position in the community, as to who would go with us and who wouldn't, and we felt that the main support for the anti-police uprising that was imminent on 3rd Street where we were having our street meetings were not the Puerto Rican people . . . we knew the kids very well, who belonged to a couple of gangs on the East Side, who came to our meetings with their stickball bats and everything, really ready for action—we did not go ahead. We said to them, we're going to give as much support as possible to Harlem, but we're not going to make it a provocation . . . We felt that we could not carry an action through with any kind of success or value, other than a blood bath . . . If the opportunity comes again—the big question is how to consolidate whatever gains are made."

Milt Rosen went on to interject the fact that PL had not created as much of an uproar as possible because "we didn't lay the groundwork and when it happened we were weak." He later made the bizarre statement that once the revolution arrived, "I'll be a black man in Harlem."

When the tension had begun to die down, Epton again tried to spur Harlem, with a public march, to new heights of anger. But before he could get the crowd moving, he was arrested by the city police and landed in jail as a result of his activities during this period.

Harlem is only a part of the case against Progressive Labor. Many of us who were considered "trustworthy" members of Progressive Labor were informed by Milt Rosen, directly prior to the Harlem fracas, that a police crackdown might be imminent. We were secretly divided into groups of four individuals each, and all were told that at the prearranged signal we would "go underground." In other words, we would drop out of sight, shed our present identities as much as possible, move into new quarters, align ourselves with the revolutionary groups in Harlem, prepare an "underground newspaper," and condition ourselves for what might be a long period of sub-rosa activity. We would continue to propagandize for violence, but nobody would know where the material was coming from, and we would try to recruit new revolutionaries. A complicated system of communication among the people and the various groups of four was arranged. In order for my group to prepare the "underground newspaper," we were to steal the needed materials. Each of the four of us was given $300 to keep us until we could raise some money "underground." This money came from the bundle the Cubans gave us for the summer trips to that socialist tourist trap.

At a meeting of my group and Milt Rosen, which took place at a park on the East River and 14th Street, we were informed that a number of pistols had been brought up from the South and that each of us would be given a pistol for protection or to use in case of arrest. These guns were later divided among the group leaders, and each of them secured a hiding place in the city for these weapons. The leader of my group asked me to find a suitable place for target practice and also a place to hide the guns. He later showed me a camera case in which the guns had been secreted in foam rubber. After I reported back that I could not find suitable places for either purpose, three of the leaders of PL attempted to bury some guns on an estate in New Castle, New York. Surprised by the local police, they beat a hasty retreat, and the police never bothered to search the cases the three were carrying.

We remained in groups of four until late August, when the program was disbanded. At least one group did go "underground" for about a week or ten days, but it was exhumed when one of its members was needed to teach at a PL training school soon to begin.

This was the first "underground" operation that I became acquainted with in Progressive Labor. The second was divulged late in the fall of 1964. In November I was approached by Fred Jerome and Jake Rosen with the proposition that I join a small group of ten and begin serious training to go "underground" permanently. A small group was being considered at that time because this operation held a "top priority and top secret" sticker, and only a limited number were to be trained at a time.

The project was discussed at a number of meetings we held in various quiet restaurants throughout the city. At each meeting, a bit more of the project was explained, until the full picture emerged in December. The plan was to train a small group (more were to be involved later) in the techniques of disguise, forgery, wiretapping, karate, and the evasion of surveillance. An apartment had been located where classes in these techniques would take place. My immediate task was to master the electronic procedures to determine whether the apartment was "bugged" and the phone tapped. Each candidate in the program was to learn a specific skill needed in the program and teach it to the others involved.

Those in this program were told that anyone who joined would have to give up his home, his belongings, and his family and to begin a new life. Project members could not marry while underground, and could never meet with known Progressive

Labor members. Finally, we were told that "there is a point where there is no turning back." Fred Jerome told me that Progressive Labor was in a position to place me in whatever occupation I chose when I went underground. I jokingly suggested that I become a priest. Without cracking a smile, Jerome told me that although they had already promised this disguise to someone else, I could have it if I really wanted it.

At this very meeting, Jake Rosen told me I would also have to go abroad for further instruction in underground work. It can only be logically assumed that work abroad included schools in terrorism and espionage. When I pressed Jake for the name of the country, he winkingly acknowledged, "There are only two where you can get the right training." He meant China and Cuba. After considerable soul-searching and conversations with a few friends who were not Communists, I decided this was nothing I wanted to be involved in.

(I could also recall previous PL schemes which had bordered on farce. One of the more "revolutionary" projects of Progressive Labor came about in the Spring of 1963. This project also had the distinction of having the shortest life-span of any PL activity and was a crowning failure. Levi Laub, along with Steve Martinot and Jake Rosen, took a truckload of guns and clothing to the miners in Hazard, Kentucky.

(Hazard had long been the center of labor trouble between the workers and the union and owners. By 1963 the scene had blown open, and the workers were actively fighting against corrupt union bosses and mineowners. The top leadership of Progressive Labor decided that Kentucky was perfect for a "war of liberation." The three revolutionaries traveled to Hazard and tried to arm the miners, set up a "revolutionary newspaper," and lead the revolution. These premature revolutionaries suddenly found themselves in hazard in Hazard—the miners threw them out, and Jake Rosen almost got shot for his efforts.)

During this period the Progressive Labor vehicle for opposing "American imperialism" throughout the world and winning new recruits was the May Second Movement, which gained its name following a demonstration in New York City on that date in 1964. The abbreviation "M-2-M" was adopted.

May Second was the offspring of a Milt Rosen speech at the Yale University Socialist Conference in March 1964. Rosen called on those assembled to form a "united front" against American presence in Vietnam. Following this speech, a group was set up to lead a demonstration against the war in Vietnam in New York on May 2nd.

Russell Stetler, at one time an independent from Haverford College, Pennsylvania, was chosen to lead the May Second Committee. Stetler was already getting attention through the Medical Aid to the Vietcong project, which he initiated and headed. His stand as an independent radical and his close relations with the Left's elder statesman, Bertrand Russell, made him a perfect front man for the M-2-M.

Levi Laub of PL and Peter Camejo of the Trotskyist Young Socialist Alliance were chosen as "coordinators" of the May 2nd anti-Vietnam war demonstration. The stationery letterhead for this demonstration listed some PL people, but most were independents with a smattering of Students for a Democratic Society. (All of the independents and SDS people withdrew after complete takeover by PL.)

As soon as the committee was set up, the operation for the demonstration began. Camejo was quickly displaced when PL refused to tell him of meetings, decisions, and plans. PL took care of the printing, advertising, and leaflet distribution. The speakers were chosen by PL, and the only people who knew what was going on in May Second were Progressive Labor people.

Fred Jerome drew up a set of proposals turning the *ad hoc* May Second committee into a permanent organization. He turned the proposals over to Levi Laub, Stetler, and me at a luncheon meeting on May 2nd shortly before the demonstration was to begin. His proposals were read by Levi Laub before the group assembled in a New York hotel, following the demonstration, and were accepted. M-2-M became institutionalized.

The "National Coordinating Committee" that was formed swiftly fell under PL's grip. Eleven of the thirteen members of this committee were members of PL, although only three were publicly known to the members. It was ridiculous. A group of us would meet privately as the PL "club" in M-2-M, decide policy, then meet with the two non-PL members, and arrive at the same decisions in their presence and with their participation.

M-2-M held two demonstrations in Times Square during August 1964, and both turned into riots. Seventeen persons were found guilty of disorderly conduct after the first riot, and almost fifty people were arrested at the second demonstration on August 15. The police saved us from starting the riot ourselves on August 8 by moving in and arresting the participants. But if the police hadn't moved in, we were prepared to foment our own trouble. A short time before this demonstration, I met with Milt Rosen, Fred Jerome, and Levi Laub in front of the PL printing company, where we discussed the strategy to be used at the demonstration. Rosen and Jerome wanted a confrontation with the police and told Laub and me to create one if necessary. Times Square had previously been declared by the police "off limits" for any political demonstrations. If the police allowed us to demonstrate, we would then attempt to lead the demonstrators out into the street and have them obstruct traffic and cause a provocation to, and a confrontation with, the police.

We regrouped the following Saturday, and when some PL members refused to follow police directives, another turmoil was created. But these arrests, including the imprisonment of Ed Lemansky for trying to strangle a policeman, only put a damper on M-2-M activities. Although the group did not invade Times Square with a demonstration for the next year, it adopted other equally agitational tactics, similar to those of the Berkeley students, but with less success.

During the late spring of 1965, M-2-M demonstrations at Columbia University, City College of New York, and Brooklyn College tried to provoke a Berkeley-type incident. The Columbia M-2-M chapter, led by PL troubleshooters and "professional students" Laub and Lemansky, spearheaded a demonstration against university exercises honoring the Reserve Officers Training Corps (ROTC). Laub and other PL stalwarts, who donned M-2-M labels for M-2-M activities, were seen there carrying pies to throw at the ROTC participants. As the demonstration verged on a riot, the university brought in the city police to break it up. The university took some disciplinary action against the student demonstrators, but the PL agitators, most of whom were not connected with the university, got off scot-free.

Rick Rhoades, a PL member representing M-2-M at CCNY, led a group of students into the Administration Building and attempted a student sit-in against the administration's educational contribution to the "military-industrial complex" of the Vietnam war; they wanted to force a call for the police to arrest the demonstrators. He tried the same tactic used at Berkeley, but with no success. Rhoades traveled to Havana in January 1966 to attend the Cuban Communist-sponsored "Tri-Continental Conference" as the representative of Progressive Labor. Upon his return to the United States later in the month, he gave a number of secret reports on that conference and on various guerrilla-warfare techniques to PL members.

At Brooklyn College, President Harry Gideonse, a long-time foe of Communism, charged that Communists were behind the recent demonstrations on his campus. The leaders of the student protest movement at Brooklyn denied these charges, but the M-2-M proudly proclaimed its role.

By 1966, with its May 2nd Movement dead, Progressive Labor began looking for a new youth forum. With its nasty reputation of trying to "out-Mao" Mao Tse Tung, and its well known liking for Stalinist-type authority, PL realized that any attempt to create a new organization would fail for lack of a decent-sized following. Accordingly, Progressive Labor set its sights on Students for a Democratic Society. Here was a ready-made target: an established youth organization with a large following. All that was necessary was for PL to move into the largest and most important SDS chapters, win control and eventually take over the national structure of SDS.

Fortunately for Progressive Labor the largest SDS chapters were located in regions where most of the PL muscle was centered: Boston, New York, and the Bay Area in California.

In New York, PL tried, but couldn't quite overcome the influence of Columbia SDS leader and soon-to-be Weatherman leader Mark Rudd.

Progressive Labor couldn't pull off an SDS take over in California either. Bay Area revolutionaries are simply too independently radical to tolerate the Stalinist control exercised by PL.

Boston, however, was another story entirely. PL moved into the Harvard SDS chapter and through sheer numerical strength won control of the chapter. It was not a case of Progressive Labor succeeding in ideological conversion of Harvard SDS members. It was simply a matter of PL being able to out-vote other factions.

The results were predictable, and served as a warning of things to come for Progressive Labor and SDS. Non-PL radicals in Harvard SDS simply left the organization. PL was left with what it had to begin with: A cadre of Progressive Labor members seeking to take over SDS. This should have indicated to PL that any attempt to take over national SDS would be nothing more than the Harvard experience magnified.

Through Harvard SDS, Progressive Labor established its well-deserved reputation of being an organization without sound ideological commitment or a specific program for action. It became a group relying on absolute demagogy to make its presence felt.

At Harvard, PL succeeded in shouting down the then Secretary of Defense Robert McNamara during one of his appearances there. Progressive Labor also involved itself in student strikes and building take overs at Harvard.

Having made a name for itself, PL closed ranks and marched off to Chicago in June, 1969, with every hope of seizing national control of SDS.

Progressive Labor came very close to having a numerical majority at the 1969 SDS national convention. But regardless of PL strength, the outcome would have been the same: Non-PL radicals in SDS would not have tolerated *any* PL influence. The result, of course, was the destruction of SDS. Non-PL'ers in SDS grouped together for the sole purpose of ejecting the Maoists. Calling themselves the Revolutionary Youth

Movement—a wide assortment of anti-Progressive Labor radicals—non-PL'ers adopted a resolution calling for the expulsion of Progressive Labor from SDS.

As might be expected, PL refused to leave SDS and indeed maintained that its followers were the only "true" Students for a Democratic Society.

In the aftermath, anti-Progressive Labor forces within SDS split into two main factions: Weatherman and Revolutionary Youth Movement II. Thus PL forces constituted the only faction retaining the name of SDS. Even today, Progressive Labor's youth group calls itself SDS.

Frequently, "worker-student alliance" is tacked on to the initials SDS. This indicates the PL-SDS philosophy that only a revolutionary force of students led by workers can create the second American revolution.

In the summer of 1969, after successfully demolishing SDS, Progressive Labor, through its youthful followers, created a public scare by announcing a program of "work-ins" whereby SDS members would infiltrate the labor forces of major industries and radicalize the workers. Much of the public alarm was due to that fact that SDS was still regarded as an organization capable of mobilizing tens of thousands of militant students instead of the 1200 or so Maoists that it actually could.

If the "work-ins" were at all successful it is certainly not evident from the PL-SDS strength found today.

In the past two years, Progressive Labor and its Students for a Democratic Society have had one brief flirtation with taking over other organizations. In July, 1970, PL and SDS showed up at a convention of the National Peace Action Coalition in Cleveland and attempted to exert influence. Their lack of numerical strength prevented any results.

"Ideologically," Progressive Labor and SDS keep plugging away at the theme of a "worker-student alliance." PL still follows much of the Chinese "political line." When Red China found fault with the Cuban revolution, so did PL and SDS. With the exception of the "worker-student alliance" theme, PL and SDS are usually found exclaiming the need to "support ghetto rebellions" such as the Harlem and Watts insurrections.

Carrying their "ideology" to ridiculous extremes, Progressive Labor and Students for a Democratic Society have condemned North Vietnam for agreeing to hold peace talks in Paris. At a mass meeting in Cleveland on June 19, 1970, a Progressive Labor spokesman said that the Vietnamese NLF (Viet Cong) were "revisionist sellouts" and that Cambodia's former premier Norodom Sihanouk was a "CIA agent." This type of rhetoric, let alone "logic," is a bit heavy-handed even for the left-wing of the 1970's.

More recently PL and Students for a Democratic Society have turned toward the Maoist dictum that political power grows out of the barrel of a gun. Realizing that it is totally incapable of winning recruits through rational discourse and thus advancing its standing among leftists, the PL-SDS combination appears to be leaning toward physical violence.

On May 26, 1971, PL and SDS disrupted a New York City budget hearing. When police moved in to remove the disrupters, PL'ers and SDS'ers resorted to brute force as a political tactic.

A similar situation was found on July 4, 1971, when members of Progressive Labor and SDS disrupted a convention of the National Peace Action Coalition and then proceeded to physically attack New York City policemen.

At present, PL and SDS are remarkably similar to early Weatherman. Both lack a sound ideology and realistic program. Both are outcasts from the New Left. As with Weatherman, PL and SDS believe that any leftist organization not controlled by them should be destroyed. And finally, PL and SDS are resorting to violence.

Ultimately Progressive Labor and its youth group will fade as organizational structures. Recruits are hard to come by for both groups. Factional struggles are tearing at the organizations from within. Some PL'ers and SDS'ers will advance to a more violent stage and perhaps go "underground" as did Weatherman. Most, however, will remain on the radical scene, not necessarily as members of Progressive Labor or Students for a Democratic Society, but certainly as Maoist demagogues calling for a "worker-student alliance."

SDS—STUDENTS FOR A DEMOCRATIC SOCIETY

ORIGINALLY, the Students for a Democratic Society (SDS) *was* the "new" left. What passes for SDS today has no relationship or relevance to what began in 1960. I was not a member of the early SDS. I wish I had been (if only to save myself from the absurdity of Progressive Labor), but because I was not, my observations are necessarily second-hand.

The person who should actually be writing this chapter is Carl Oglesby, a founder of SDS and a man both troubled and profound. Oglesby played a leading role in the early formation of SDS and is the only leader of that period (whom I know) still committed to the goals inherent within that "new" left movement.

The difficulty with dealing with SDS is perspective. Obviously, from the outset, SDS was not concerned with many of the goals that most Americans desire. A basic plank in their ideology was socialism, and this is inherently abhorent to those of us who believe in the concept of free will and laissez-faire capitalism. Still, the point of perspective is important. There are too many devil theories as things exist. The last thing we need is *more* conspiracy theories of history.

No, the early SDS founders were not models of Lenin incarnate. Neither were they the all too easily identifiable weatherman type. Even Tom Hayden has changed considerably over the years, and I doubt if his now verbose utterances would have gained much following in 1960.

Students for a Democratic Society was founded in 1960 as the student arm of the League for Industrial Democracy. The League for Industrial Democracy (LID) has primarily been a moderate Socialist organization with a non-Communist ideology. LID was formed in 1905 by Upton Sinclair, J. Phelps Stokes, and Jack London.

The League for Industrial Democracy is controlled by a board of leading Democratic Socialists who lived through the "united front" period of the 1930's, the purge trials in Moscow, and subsequent Soviet imperialism. Such distinguished Democratic Socialists as Sidney Hook, Harry A. Overstreet, Louis Fischer, Jack Barbash, Mike Harrington, and Clarence Senior are included in the leadership of the LID. No one could rationally deny their non-Communist position.

When the LID decided in 1960 to form a viable youth group, they utilized the name Students for a Democratic Society. In the early years, SDS was primarily concerned with revitalizing the democratic process and was not interested in passing itself off as socialist. In fact, its early constitution had specific provisions denying Communists membership in SDS. The founding constitution of SDS described it as "an association of young people on the left" and extended an invitation to "liberals and radicals, activists and scholars, students and faculty." Then, in 1962, SDS met at Port Huron in Michigan and drew up a statement outlining immediate programs and policies. This Port Huron Statement made it obvious that SDS was antagonistic to both the totalitarianism of Communism and the programs of the Communist Party.

For the next two years, SDS had some success on the campuses of the Midwest and the border state schools. SDS was immediately appealing because it was "new" and was also approaching the problems of the 1960s in a fresh and imaginative manner. Its community action programs, its concept of participatory democracy, its concern with student governments and off-campus housing situations, its desire to deal directly with the students' own frustrations about campus life, were appealing. The discussion papers and longer position papers of SDS were the only thing of their type on either the Old or the New Left. SDS also aligned itself with a number of the protest movements against segregation and discrimination. Indeed, the Student Non-violent Coordinating Committee (SNCC) drew much of its early membership from the ranks of SDS.

Within two years, SDS began to show students that they could involve themselves in radical political activities without being Communists or totalitarian leftists. They were radical, hard working, inventive, democratic, and vital in a period when the Old Communist left had almost ruined any concept of a pragmatic approach to left-wing politics.

During this period, SDS was perhaps the strongest at the University of Michigan, where Al Haber and others set up a large, vocal chapter that was successful in exercising a strong influence on the student government there. The SDS people also came to play a significant role at the National Student Association annual meetings. In fact, SDS leaders were usually responsible for achieving whatever left-liberal changes were achieved at NSA conferences held to assess student opinion. No one would have seriously contended during this period that SDS represented any other strain than that of Democratic Socialism.

However, it was not all smooth sailing for SDS during this period. The LID periodically questioned some of the activities and policies of SDS, such as their distribution of the Communist *Monthly Review*, and even at one point in 1962 expressed their distress by cutting off funds for a short period. In fact, the financial tie between the LID and SDS was long a point of contention between them. The League for Industrial Democracy is financed by private and public money. Individual donors, however, play a far less significant financial role than do various labor unions that contribute a major part of the money needed to run the LID. Chief among the labor union contributors are the United Auto Workers, the Amalgamated Clothing Workers, and the independent District 65 of New York. Originally SDS depended heavily on the money it received from various large unions interested in a left-liberal approach to politics.

By the fall of 1964, SDS had grown into the most significant group on the New Left. It had more members and more chapters than any other New Left group, and its pragmatic approach to problems was certainly a tremendous influence on campuses across the country. At this time, SDS began a national campaign for both members and funds to carry out its program. Identical letters appeared in a number of radical and liberal publications signed by such people as the professor emeritus of the pacifist movement, A. J. Muste, the independent journalist, I. F. Stone, and W. H. "Ping" Ferry, of the Center for Democratic Institutions, a Ford Foundation operation. These letters all read, "We want to inform your readers about a critical new development on the American political scene—the emergence of an organization of students and young people who are seriously committed to building a new American left."

This was a big breakthrough for SDS. SDS had grown from approximately 200 members in 1960 to a claimed membership of 2,000 in 70 chapters in 1965. According to an article in the January 9, 1965, issue of the Old Left newspaper, the *National Guardian*, SDS "is the largest student organization on the left." At the 1965 National SDS Convention held in Kewadin, Michigan, students from a large number of campuses attended. Included in the list of represented colleges were the University of California (Berkeley), Pennsylvania State, University of Texas, Vanderbilt, Amherst, University of the South, Emory University, Florida State, University of Wisconsin, University of Oklahoma, Queens College, Columbia, Harvard, Boston College, Wayne State, Long Island University, Northwestern, Northeastern, Loyola in New Orleans, and Washington State, to note just a few.

In 1964 the SDS membership and leaders decided to devote their energies to local community problems through the country. SDS members flocked to the South to work with

SNCC in its various voter-registration projects, thereby giving SNCC a New Left radicalism that separated it from the rest of the civil-rights movement.

This radicalism was exemplified when John Lewis, a one-time leader of SNCC, announced in early January of 1966 that they supported efforts by young Americans who "are unwilling to respond to a military draft." The SNCC leadership drafted a statement accusing the United States government of aggression in South Vietnam and stating that "The United States government has never guaranteed the freedom of oppressed citizens and is not yet truly determined to end the rule of terror and oppression within its own borders."

SDS also decided to go into the ghettos of a number of American cities and work with the underprivileged in a program of "participatory democracy." SDS members seemed determined to develop the poor into a political force in this country. Contrary to the Communists, they decided that it was more important to move into the ghetto areas to live themselves than to flood these areas with "working-class literature." At least ten such ghetto projects were started by SDS: Baltimore, Chicago, Cleveland, Newark, San Francisco, Cambridge (Maryland), Roxbury (Massachusetts), Chester (Pennsylvania), Cairo (Illinois) and Appalachia. SDS also set up a coordinating section, called the Economic Research and Education Project (ERAP), in Ann Arbor, Michigan, to oversee all of these activities.

Perhaps the most successful, and controversial, ERAP project was in Newark, New Jersey. According to the 1965 SDS National Convention, this project was the only one to achieve any significant progress, while most other ERAP efforts were folding. The Newark Community Union Project (NCUP) was headed by a former SDS president, Tom Hayden, who was unquestionably one of the smartest and best qualified of the young SDS members. Tom Hayden helped draft the original Port Huron Statement, and at various National Student Association conferences was one of the most rational and convincing of the SDS representatives.

The radical approach of Hayden and his companions to rent control, tighter code enforcement, prosecution of absentee landlords, and an end to "collusion" between welfare workers and slumlords, culminated in a number of well-publicized picket lines and rent strikes. These actions angered the regular politicians of the community even more, and charges flew fast and furious between the city council and NCUP.

The problem of urban renewal was the key to action in Newark. SDS opposed the program, claiming it would simply remove the poor from the area and replace them with middle-class housing projects. According to an article in the September 27, 1965, issue of the *New Leader*, the NCUP sought a reversal of the urban renewal project's direction. We want the people to control it." The slogan of the NCUP was "Give the people control of urban renewal." SDS, however, was not working to increase the political effectiveness of the ghetto people in Newark, and Hayden stated that he considers voter registration as being "of questionable importance." He was not, however, at all clear as to how to institute his program without the increased political participation of the Negroes in the ghetto. It is now obvious that he was simply disdainful of the democratic procedures of voting and had mass action and civil disobedience in mind.

In 1966 Hayden had abandoned the original SDS concept of avoiding cooperation with Communists. He travelled illegally to North Vietnam in the company of Herbert Aptheker, the Communist Party's chief theoretician.

SDS used the phrase "participatory democracy" as indicative of its ultimate goal for all Americans. This plan resembles a type of mass "town meeting" where the so-called unrepresented elements of our society would have their say in all political questions. Unfortunately, this romance with the idea of "participatory democracy" overshadowed the proposal of any concrete programs. It became just a catchphrase.

By 1965, SDS was compelled to admit that they had made relatively little inroad into the problems of the ghetto. Most of their community action programs had either folded or were operating with typical radical inefficiency. A major reason for the failure of SDS to spur the poor into a realization of their destiny as a "revolutionary force" in this country was the lack of both means and ends. One of the inevitable consequences of sending middle-class students into ghetto areas is the immediate disparity between the helpers and those to be helped. No matter how hard these young rebels tried to acclimate themselves to the community, it was a rare case when they were accepted as anything more than temporary allies against the slumlords or the welfare agencies. After all, these young students were not an endemic part of the ghetto and were at liberty to flee back to the relative isolation and security of the middle class. Other problems dealt with language and color. Most of the SDS workers were white and did not speak Spanish and were therefore isolated even more from a significant sector of the ghetto they were trying to reach.

Community organizing eventually gave way to other tactics. The Vietnam war began to escalate in 1965 and SDS felt the need to step in and take a leadership role in opposition to that war.

SDS initiated the first mass demonstrations against Vietnam involvement, but in doing so adopted the "united front" concept in an effort to mobilize sentiment against the war. No longer were Communists and other totalitarian radicals excluded from SDS ranks. The united front opened the way for every power-hungry vulture on the American Left to march into SDS and attempt to flex some muscle.

This became the ultimate undoing of SDS. With the organization's decentralized structure, the SDS national office was powerless to clean house in local chapters.

Numerous opposing political tendencies continued to enter SDS with an eye on grabbing complete control of the organization. Internal feuds quickly developed, and SDS, as a result, lost control of the anti-war movement to groups such as the Spring Mobilization Committee and the National Mobilization Committee.

Hard core radical elements succeeded in winning control of important local SDS chapters. During 1967-69, when SDS was at its zenith, radical leadership succeeded in turning student frustration over the war into militant action such as university building take-overs and the complete shut-down of Columbia University.

SDS sealed its fate when it invited *all* leftists to participate in the united front. It was an open invitation for all totalitarian elements on the left to participate in the destruction of SDS from within.

As early as 1965, Progressive Labor, with its own youth group on the wane, began to lay plans for the infiltration and eventual control of SDS.

PL lacked the concentrated numerical power necessary to take over any great number of SDS chapters, but when combined at a national SDS convention PL was aware that its forces would come very close to having a majority.

The national office of SDS realized that Progressive Labor stood as a devisive force within the organization, but it was trapped in the classic conundrum. On the one hand, the national office had invited the Maoists of Progressive Labor to rest within the movement bed. On the other hand, the pragmatic evidence showed that once inside, PL was about to rape the very people that had so liberally opened the sheets.

The curtain fell in Chicago at the 1969 SDS National Convention. The Progressive Labor heavies squared off against two other factions within SDS: one group led by the soon-to-be outgoing SDS national secretary Mike Klonsky, the other led by the soon-to-be Weatherman leaders Mark Rudd and Bernadine Dohrn.

With the anti-PL members split two ways, Progressive Labor would have had little trouble controlling the convention. Unfortunately for PL, however, the two anti-Maoist factions managed to team up long enough to agree that Progressive Labor should once and for all be ejected from SDS.

Meeting in caucus and calling itself the Revolutionary Youth Movement, the two anti-PL factions agreed that PL had to go. The caucus ended when Bernadine Dohrn declared, "We are not a caucus. We are SDS."

The anti-PL'ers returned to convention hall and read Progressive Labor out of SDS.

Progressive Labor would hear of no such thing. It retained the name of Students for a Democratic Society.

With the PL question supposedly settled, the anti-Maoist caucus returned to its own feud. The ultimate result was another split within SDS: The Weathermen, led by Mark Rudd,

Bernadine Dohrn, Jeff Jones and Bill Ayers versus the Revolutionary Youth Movement II (RYM-II) led by Mike Klonsky and Les Coleman.

Weatherman ran off with the SDS mailing lists, the money, the top leadership and retained possession of SDS national headquarters at 1608 W. Madison Street in Chicago.

Weatherman, which for all practical purposes is now defunct, will be detailed in a later chapter.

RYM-II made one futile stab at establishing a name for itself. In October of 1969 it called on radicals to come to Chicago to protest the closing of an International Harvester plant on the city's South Side. Several hundred RYM-II followers invaded Mayor Daley's turf, only to be out-publicized by the Weatherman "Days of Rage" which were being held at the same time.

In early 1970, a RYM-II faction opposing the Klonsky-Coleman leadership called a meeting in Atlanta. The result was the formation of RYM-III. Neither group has been heard from since.

Progressive Labor elements are the only forces still using the name Students for a Democratic Society. Known also as the Worker-Student Alliance, the PL-SDS faction has most of its strength on the East Coast—notably Boston—but is opening up some interest on the West Coast.

The final result of the pre-1969 united front policy of SDS is that the only existing SDS is now Progressive Labor, which means quite simply that SDS is presently an extension of the most repressive elements of the communist ideology.

The demise of Students for a Democratic Society has resulted in a nostalgia among many liberal students with whom I visit, for they seem to realize that what was envisioned is not what has come to pass.

"YOU DON'T NEED A WEATHERMAN..."

8

THE public now identifies SDS and Weatherman in the same mental picture. To most people, the split at the 1969 SDS national convention never happened. The Weatherman faction of SDS has captured the spotlight and the other factions are relatively unheard of except in specialized political journals.

The Weathermen resemble the Visigoth cometh. The Weathermen are like the Kamikaze pilots on the late movies. The Weathermen believe the revolution is upon us and that they are in the vanguard of the revolution. The Weathermen are true narodniks.

Living in collectives, reading the same literature, leading Spartan lives, resisting martyrdom, hating the bourgeoise, loving the lumpen proletariat, the Weathermen have carved out a unique niche in radical history. The public stereotype could only portray the Weathermen as long frocked, flop hatted, bearded and hairy anarchists with a bomb in one hand and a black revolver in the other.

111

But the Weathermen dispel the image because many of them whom I have met look more like the stereotype of totally "bourgeoise" workers rather than hippies or anarchists. In fact, the Weathermen are among the straightest looking people on the radical scene.

At a Denver University debate, I was opposed by a Weatherman fill-in for Bill Ayers who was under federal indictment for criminal conspiracy. The Weatherman I debated, along with his female bodyguards, were closer characterizations of "criminal types" than hippies or long-haired anarchists. They wore black jackets, white cotton socks, made an issue of using foul language, and spoke as if they were imitating the shouts of bygone street vendors. The Weatherwomen were type cast as fishmongers and their language was only outdistanced by their screeches.

In this particular debate, my Weatherman opponent declared that he wanted to see the United States dominated by a communist government and that force and violence are acceptable means to reach that end. I can only relate that the audience was stunned. After a rambling session interrupted by a couple of near fist fights, the Weathermen began shouting about the need for revolution. My wife was standing by herself in the back of the auditorium holding our three month old son, Dylan. After the fracas, a militant Weatherwoman approached her with the crack: "Hey, is that Luce's brat?"

Barbra replied that indeed Dylan was our child. The Weatherwoman threw back her head and shouted, "F_ _ _ _' ugly kid, ain't he?"

At this juncture, a number of people who would not have normally become involved in the interaction between two unfamiliar people became interested and emoted a feeling of disgust for the callous level to which someone would sink in order to attempt to make a political point.

The name "Weatherman" was taken from a line in a Bob Dylan song relating to the fact that "you don't need a weatherman to know which way the wind blows." In the case of the political Weathermen you need a program to keep up with their various battles and terrorist attacks.

The Weatherman organization was created as a result of the

Progressive Labor attempt to take over the last national SDS convention in Chicago, Illinois. The Weatherman faction is, in reality, much of the old national staff of SDS, among others. The leaders of Weatherman now are Mark Rudd, who made a name for himself as the *enfant terrible* at Columbia University and Bernadine Dohrn, a lawyer and radical feminist. Miss Dohrn has not only publicly praised Charles Manson, but is reported to have told a Weatherman conclave that she was ecstatic because she and other Weatherpeople had recently walked up and down the aisles of an airplane simply taking food off people's plates. The remarkable thing, of course, about her narrative is the fact that the passengers simply allowed Miss Dohrn and her childish followers to play such games.

The Weathermen have been involved in a little bit of everything. Their more publicized actions have taken place in Chicago, Boston, and Washington.

In Chicago, the Weathermen decided to liberate the city through a proposed program of high school "jailbreaks" and a city-wide scattering of "wargasams." The over-all Chicago action was publicized by Weatherman as the "Days of Rage" and was held October 8-11, 1969.

For several weeks prior to the "Days of Rage" Weathermen chieftains, notably Rudd, Dohrn, Ayers, Jeff Jones, and Charles "Chip" Marshall, made the rounds of campuses where SDS chapters existed or once existed. Weatherman urged students to come to Chicago prepared to do battle with police. A turn-out of thousands was predicted by the Weatherman hierarchy. In reality, only hundreds showed up for the riot.

That poor turn-out is best explained by a "debate" held at Indiana University prior to the "Days of Rage." Mark Rudd squared off against Les Coleman of the RYM II-SDS faction. Coleman had come to Indiana to promote a RYM II demonstration in opposition to the closing of an International Harvester plant in Chicago. The RYM II action was to be in direct competition with the "Days of Rage."

When the Rudd-Coleman shouting stopped, one leftist in the audience rose to dash the hopes of both: "As for you Les Coleman, I'm sorry that plant will close and put people out of work. I hope you Chicago people can do something about it. I plan to work on some of the problems in Indiana before I worry about Chicago. As for you Mark Rudd, if you think I'm going to Chicago to get my skull cracked for the glory of Weatherman, then you're out of your mind." Thunderous applause.

If Les Coleman couldn't get people to Chicago for what may have been a legitimate cause then Mark Rudd had no hope of getting them there for a sound beating at the hands of the Chicago police.

The "angry masses" failed to materialize in Chicago but the Weathermen faithful turned out. The predicted thousands melted into hundreds, but the spirit of the day overcame the paucity of the number. Armed with crash helmets, rags soaked in water (to dispel the effects of tear gas), army boots, light weight clothes, chains, baseball bats and no apparent fear, the modern day Mongol horde arrived on Mayor Daley's pavement.

The "Days of Rage" were pitiful to all involved. Oh, there were red flags, Viet Cong chants, and plenty of damage to property, but Weatherman stock among the radical community plummeted. The Weatherpeople could only mobilize a couple of voices of support from the left-wing radical element. Tom Hayden managed to give a few words of encouragement. Jerry Rubin said he couldn't really fault the Weathermen. More important, however, the "Days of Rage" succeeded in alienating important radical groups from Weatherman. The Black Panthers, one of the black groups to which Weatherman had dedicated the "Days of Rage," supported the competing RYM-II action and accused the Weathermen of "Custerism," which means the Weathermen had the mentality of kamikaze pilots.

The Weatherpeople proved the Panthers correct. They shouted, they provoked, they ranted and they were arrested.

The Weathermen ran amuck on occasion and did considerable damage to cars and windows but in the end they were subdued without much violence on either side.

A Bernadine Dohrn-led march of Weatherwomen had the announced purpose of destroying the Chicago military induction center. A few Chicago policemen simply formed a semi-circle around the girls and ushered them into a subway station. Many of the Weatherwomen broke into tears.

Boston was also hit by the "Days of Rage." Several Weatherwomen invaded a couple of high schools and managed to frighten most of the kids and all of the teachers. They physically bound and gagged one teacher while using karate to keep the students in place.

The whole thing boiled down to an enforced teach-in in which only one side was presented. The Weatherwomen told the students their side of the question on revolution and heaven protect the infidel that might attempt a protest. The dissenter was immediately subjected to the reality of karate.

After the "Days of Rage" Westherman turned to its new targets: Washington, D.C., and the New Mobilization Committee which had called for a Washington demonstration to protest the war.

Weatherman attempted to extort $10,000 from the "New Mobe" in return for a pledge of no Weatherman violence at the November demonstration in Washington.

The New Mobe refused to knuckle under and Weatherman went on a rampage during the demonstration. Extensive damage was done at the Justice Dept., the South Vietnamese Embassy, and on sections of Connecticut Avenue.

Weatherman spent the next month licking its wounds. The Weatherman thinking during this cooling off period was that the political climate had become more repressive. The leftists of the anti-war movement ("peace creeps" in Weatherman terminology) couldn't be counted on for support. Even the Panthers had copped out on Weatherman. What was needed was an underground terrorist organization, an organization consisting largely of white bomb throwers who could be counted on to create a diversion while militant Blacks prepared for outright revolution.

With this in mind Weatherman called a "National War Council" in Flint, Michigan, December 27-30, 1969.

Some 400 of the super-radicals made their appearance at a hall decked with a huge cardboard machine gun. To chants of "Off the Pig," "Sirhan Sirhan Power," and "Charlie Manson

Power," Weatherman met publicly for the last time and decided to go underground.

Shortly after the Flint "War Council," a Federal Grand Jury in Chicago handed up indictments against leading Weathermen for their part in the Chicago "Days of Rage": Mark Rudd, Bernadine Dohrn, Bill Ayers, Howard Machtinger, John Jacobs, Linda Sue Evans, Cathy Wilkerson, Kathie Boudin, and Judith Clark.

With Weatherman already underground and the indictments creating even more "repression," Weatherman struck back at "pig Amerika" with a bombing wave.

Banks, police stations, and corporate offices were destroyed by Weatherman bombs.

In New York, the whole course of Weatherman insanity took shape.

When an explosion demolished a $275,000 townhouse at 18 West 11th St., on Friday, March 6, 1970, the blast gained headlines mainly because actor Dustin Hoffman, who occupied one of the neighboring Greenwich Village homes, managed to rescue a few of his paintings and a valuable Tiffany lamp.

At first New York City police officials assumed the cause of the explosions and resulting fire to have been a gas leak. Their immediate concern was to locate two young women who were seen rushing naked from the scene.

The press was interested in the explosion because the house belonged to James P. Wilkerson, the owner of a chain of radio stations in the Midwest.

As the authorities began a routine probe of the ruins—the explosion almost totally destroyed the four-story house and ripped a huge hole in the front and side of the renovated townhouse - they discovered that something was amiss.

Almost immediately after their search started, firemen unearthed the body of a young man, later identified as Theodore Gold. A 23-year-old former Columbia University student, he had been an active member of Students for a Democratic Society (SDS) and had served on the organization's Steering Committee during the time of the 1968 Columbia student strike.

After leaving Columbia, Gold became further radicalized. He

visited Cuba with a select group of SDS activists. While on the Communist-controlled island, these traveling revolutionaries conferred with representatives from the Vietnamese National Liberation Front (the Viet Cong). Upon his return to the United States, Gold attended the SDS National Convention held in Chicago and turned into a Weatherman.

Following the discovery of Gold's body, the police surmised that one of the women seen fleeing the scene was none other than Cathlyn Wilkerson, daughter of the owner of the demolished townhouse and herself a Weatherman. She had been arrested in sundry SDS demonstrations and had participated in the Chicago fracas.

(At the time of the explosion in her father's home she was free on $40,000 bail as a result of her activities in Chicago. Previous to her involvement with Weatherman, Miss Wilkerson had edited "New Left Notes," the SDS newsletter. She had also served as a member of the SDS Interim Council.)

As workmen continued to sort through the debris, they accumulated more and more evidence indicating that the townhouse had served as a bomb factory for young radicals. Neighbors noted that several young people had been regularly seen leaving and entering the house during Mr. Wilkerson's absence. As the search of the ruins progressed, a large number of SDS leaflets and pamphlets was found. In addition, various identification and credit cards of a number of known radicals were discovered in the rubble.

On Tuesday, March 10, 1970, the torso of a young woman was recovered from the wreckage. Later in the day, a total of 57 sticks of dynamite, four 12-inch pipes crudely packed with explosives, 30 blasting caps and other bomb-making apparatus were discovered in the water-filled basement in what appeared to have been a workshop area.

The police also discovered that the radicals were surrounding the dynamite bombs with nails. In other words, they were not simply making bombs to destroy private property, but were making anti-personnel bombs that would be used to kill people.

Later police positively identified Cathlyn Wilkerson as one of the two women seen running from the house and still at large. They also speculated that the second woman might have been

Kathy Boudin, a close friend of Miss Wilkerson. Several purses containing credit cards and identification belonging to Miss Boudin were found in the debris.

Kathy Boudin is the only daughter of Leonard Boudin, a left-wing lawyer who represented the other three organizers of the 1963 and 1964 trips to Cuba. Mr. Boudin is the "registered" attorney for the Cuban Communist government in the United States and also a lawyer for Dr. Benjamin Spock and other radicals.

Miss Boudin has an interesting background in New Left activism. She spent 15 months in the Soviet Union while a student at Bryn Mawr, but became disillusioned with Russian youths who were skeptical of her analysis of the "repression" in the United States.

Since her return to this country, she has been a co-chairman of the conference on the Second American Revolution and has co-authored a variety of articles addressed to young radicals on the legal system. She was named a co-conspirator in the federal indictment against the notorious "Chicago 7" and with Miss Wilkerson was scheduled to appear in Chicago on charges stemming from their participation in Weatherman's "Days of Rage."

When the two girls did not appear before the criminal court in Chicago, the court ordered their bail revoked and issued a warrant for their arrest for unlawful flight to avoid prosecution. The Federal Bureau of Investigation was then asked to enter the case. Both women can now be arrested under federal jurisdiction without additional charges being filed. The judge also reset bail for both at $75,000.

As work continued in the townhouse debris, the torso of the woman's body previously uncovered was identified as Diana Oughton. A little finger discovered in the ruins was the key to her identification. The 28-year-old Illinois native was also a Weatherwoman activist and had been arrested during the Chicago demonstrations held in October of 1969. Diana was the girlfriend of Bill Ayers, educational secretary of the Weatherman faction. Both Diana Oughton and Ayers are the children of well-to-do Illinois businessmen.

Another body, that of Terry Robbins, was identified.

The police theorized that the bombs being made in the townhouse basement were to be used at Columbia University during an SDS demonstration. The student radicals were demanding that the university trustees put up the $1 million bail for the Black Panthers who were facing trial for attempting to blow up a number of New York department stores the Saturday prior to Easter 1969.

The tragedy of the New York bomb explosion is not that it was the work of a bunch of wealthy kids gone suddenly insane, but that the campaign of terror in this nation reached the point where youthful zealots were making anti-personnel bombs.

Suddenly in late 1970 the bombings stopped. Bernadine Dohrn sent a "weather report" to the Liberation News Service in New York. Dohrn's remarks revealed a Weatherman consensus that the bombings had not achieved the desired political results. What is needed, Dohrn said, is more mass organizing. Dohrn offered no indication as to how Weatherman would lead or participate in this new tactic.

Eventually Weathermen leaders will be arrested.

Whether or not their followers will retaliate with terrorism remains to be seen. But Weatherman will always be remembered in the annals of American radicalism for its violent ultra-leftism.

There is a lesson to be learned from Weatherman when analyzing the "second American revolution." All communist or radical organizations look forward to the day when violence and terror can be effectively used to overthrow established government. This applies to the Communist Party, the Trotskyites, Progressive Labor, any radical organization one cares to name. But the revolution must progress in stages. "Revolutionary consciousness" must be raised gradually among the populace. At the present time the public is simply not radicalized to the point of tolerating bombings. Weatherman jumped the gun, but other radical organizations look forward to the day when they can employ Weatherman's tactics successfully.

THE CRAZIES 9

THE New Left is often publicly identified with the "crazies." A cross-fertilization process between the mass media and the leftists created a hybrid type of pop star nihilist. This kind of "crazy" was personified in the public mind by a Jerry Rubin/Abbie Hoffman/ Gracie Slick collage.

Depending upon your point of political perspective, the emergence of the crazies signaled either the end or the beginning of "the revolution." The crazies have a lot going for them—they all resemble someone you knew in your childhood and hoped you might not ever run into again in adult life. The crazies are individuals like Hoffman and Rubin and groups like the Mad Dogs and the White Panthers. The crazies violate all the accepted norms: political, social, ethical, religious, psychological, etc. The crazies are out to zap the world into their own image. The crazies are convinced that the sane people are presently housed in mental insitutions and that the people on the outside should be incarcerated. The crazies are everything your mother warned you against.

To conceive of a crazy you have to recall the Dada movement in art. A political crazy can stand for anything or nothing. He or she can say anything and mean literally nothing. On the other hand, the crazy may be utilizing the political theatre of the absurd in order to attempt to drive you into new arenas of thought in order to make you see reality from a different perspective.

You really cannot pin down the crazies. The one thing that is possible to do with them is to identify the species and to try to relate a bit about their foibles. The first thing to note is that the successful crazies, like Rubin and Hoffman, are using capitalism to destroy capitalism. The fact that they both became financially successful shows something about the mentality of the American people. Few countries have indeed so openly paid and honored their destroyers.

Both Rubin and Hoffman are political anomolies. They did not come to public attention through the usual manner of publishing and political activism. They gained public attention after capturing the essence of shock theatre coupled with an understanding that television was dependent upon crazy acts for its news coverage. Both Rubin and Hoffman worked with an effective political prescription: take a country in crisis, with a youth population in revolt against the symbols of their elders, a television industry determined to pay heed to anything so long as it is outrageous and then add two political zanies. Stir the brew and add a couple of witches, a pig, some Black Panthers, a healthy pinch of liberal indecision and you have the youth hit of the era—Jerry and Abbie, both over thirty, prancing around like a couple of seven year olds to the delight of the teenagers and the dismay of the adult population. The liberals were shocked but couldn't say anything. After all, they were their children. The conservatives were just shocked. The kids loved it. Television made money off the crazies and in the process lost its soul. Jerry and Abbie are living off the fat of the land while they tell kids to murder their parents. The intellectuals in the publishing world are fascinated with the crazies and believe them to be Pied Pipers in rags. It used to be "would you want your daughter to marry a Jerry Rubin?" Now it's "why not take a Jerry Rubin to lunch?"

I cannot possibly write about all of the crazies that exist on the political spectrum left of Chairman Mao. The list will always be incomplete because it is in constant flux. Some of the crazies take themselves seriously, like Mike Lasky and his Communist Party of the United States (Marxist-Leninist). Lasky was a leader of the group (with about five members) but they had a fight and Lasky was expelled. So then there were four.

Jerry Rubin has no party but he has a following. Rubin has recently made a national name for himself both as a result of his conviction in Chicago (for his role in the riots that shook the 1968 Democratic Party's national convention) and because of his book *Do It!* Rubin is the prototype of the crazy symbol. His book is an autobiography of a crazy.

It is too easy to simply discount *Do It!* either because of the character of the author or the nihilism he espouses. Jerry Rubin may be a political malaprop but his book shows some mastery of the medium technique argued by McLuhan. In fact, *Do It!* and *Woodstock Nation* by Jerry's compatriot Abbie Hoffman very effectively utilize graphics and varied type styles to capture the would-be reader's attention.

The publisher's plug on the back of the paperback edition of *Do It!* calmly states that: "This book will become a Molotov cocktail in your hands. Jerry Rubin has written The Communist Manifesto of our era. *Do It!* is a Declaration of War between the generations—calling on kids to leave their homes, burn down their schools and create a new society upon the ashes of the old." If that rhetoric isn't enough to make you rush down to your local bookstore then it should at least make you wonder what they are smoking at Simon and Schuster.

Do It! is dedicated to "Nancy, Dope, Color TV, and Violent Revolution!" The author admonishes his audience to "read this book stoned!"—not a bad idea: then it might make sense.

The introduction to this scatology was written by Eldridge Cleaver from Algeria. The perspective that Cleaver captures in his introduction is fitting tribute to what follows. Take for example this analysis of the Democratic Convention in Chicago:

123

"This gives me a chance to put forward an alternative interpretation of the Democratic National Convention held in Chicago in August 1968.

"Most people are eager to say that the pigs flipped out, or that they finally showed their true colors. I disagree, I BELIEVE THAT WHAT HAPPENED IN Chicago is a direct result of conspiracies hatched by the Republican Party and those who supported Nixon for President, working hand in hand with the racist, right-wing John Birchers who control the Chicago police Department just as they control the police departments in many important cities throughout the country. The Rupublicans knew that they had to move in a decisive manner or risk the Democrats' winning the election by a close margin. Nixon, having lost once on a cliff-hanger, was not taking any more chances. So someone dreamed up the greedy idea of shocking the American people into fear and hysteria and at the same time both wrecking the Democratic National Convention and firmly establishing in the minds of the American people the image of the Democrats as being responsible for the violence going down in Babylon . . ."

Now there's an illuminating theory for you to chew on.

If you either buy or steal *Do It!* and find yourself in the right frame of mind it can make frightening but interesting reading. It is obviously aimed at a youth audience—Rubin claimed on the Dick Cavett program that his audience was mainly composed of seven-to nine-year-olds—and contains about all the clever and outrageous little ditties that you might expect. There is no denying Jerry is a showman.

Rubin's program is captured in the chapter head "Revolution is Theater-in-the Streets." Or—"You are the stage. You are the actor. Everything is for real. There is no audience." Or—"Looting and Shoplifting Can Get You High." Or—"Barbers will go to rehabilitation camps where they will grow their hair long."

Jerry is certainly no classical communist and he does a fair job of putting down the orthodoxy of the established American Marxist-Leninist groupings. He dislikes their structure and their insistence upon models. For Jerry there is only one mode of operation and that is to *Do It!*

Accordingly, it matters little what you do just as long as you *Do It!* Everything appears as fair game for Jerry Rubin. It is this very kind of scattergun approach to reality that makes Jerry so difficult to accept on any level.

A little bit of craziness is sort of fun until you begin to see that it masks a serious illness. If this is true in people it is even more accurate in politics. If Jerry Rubin were just nuts then he would be a menace only unto himself. And, of course, Jerry is a smidgen bats, but he is dangerous. Rubin's danger lies not in the pragmatic absurdity he espouses but in the fact that his nihilism begins to rub off on those students that are seeking something new and exciting to espouse while not having to think. And here comes Jerry with a non-plan that says that all you have to do to be a successful revolutionary is *Do It!*

To the political crazies, Rubin is a symbol. He has made it pragmatically viable to do anything and justify it as YIPPIE. That's right, folks, anyone can be a real zany and in the process destroy some private property, paint his face and make the big time New York cultural scene. Just look at Jerry—the subject of articles in *Look* and *Esquire* and the model for God knows how many bombings—and you have to *know* that this is the land of opportunity.

Rubin is being used—not in an a/b/c relationship, and certainly not wittingly, but still used. Jerry is saying that society is sick and that all you have to do to make it well is freak out—bomb it, burn it and somehow, magically, *we will all be free.*

What Jerry doesn't seem to be able to get is the fact that if we all go out and *Do It!* and smash the current state that we will end up with something quite worse. Even if successful, the anarchists are always the first to go once the revolution is consummated. The vacuum is always filled by power. Now you can argue that this is not what you wanted to see, but history does have some right to say that this is what has always happened.

Of course, I am not at all certain Rubin doesn't understand the fact that out of anarchy would come the thermador.

Although he comes on like a quasi-anarchist, Jerry is basically power oriented. There are numerous examples of how Jerry would utilize his self-appointed "truth" to force others to behave as he believed correct such as "Barbers will go to rehabilitation camps."

At one juncture in the Rubin rhetoric he admitted that the movie "Wild in the Streets" had given him a near vision. The story line in the movie deals with a teeny-bopper take over of the government with the following Nazi like "rehabilitation camp" reality for anyone over the age of thirty. No, Rubin is less an anarchist than an incipient monarchist.

I don't "hate" Jerry, but I do not trust him either. I have the feeling now, just as I did in 1964 when I sent him to Cuba, that this is a man that could really desire the spotlight of power.

He writes of me as the "poet of the Progressive Labor Party." A dubious distinction at best although I find a gleam of satisfaction in knowing that Jerry has read my poems. But then:

> "Luce has changed sides. Dig it. Luce, who had helped organize the Cuba trips and had once gone skinnydipping with Fidel, joined with the FBI and ratted on all of his friends.
>
> "It was the *only* desertion in the history of our movement. Throughout the 1940's and the 1950's Communist Party members turned up as FBI agents. Every day right-wingers and liberals become left-wingers, radicals become yippies. But in the New Left there has been only one Phillip Abbot (sic) Luce."

In the whole of *Do It!* I probably receive as much note as anyone—except, of course, Jerry. Why this hatred, this spleen letting? What is on Rubin's mind that makes him nervous when I'm around?

This naturally leads me to a story: in 1969, Rubin came out to California on a speaking tour. Having nothing better to do, my wife and I drove up to Long Beach from La Jolla in order to witness the appearance of Rubin in Southern California.

Rubin gave his then usual rap about the state and how we should tear it down with humor and violence. There he was replete with Indian head band, crossed bandoliers, war paint and Yippie. He was a clown talking to middle-class white radical students and urging them to destroy the system by painting the buildings red. And they dug it and they all laughed and shouted and kept their seats. Then Jerry told them how evil capitalism was by saying "private property is pure s_." And everyone would giggle and think it was cute to hate property 'cause Jerry said it was "in" to hate property.

When it was all over Jerry and some big body-guard type walked over to the bookstore and started "rapping" with some of the local radicals. Then it all just sort of happened.

My wife and I were walking with a friend, and we walked over to Jerry and his buddy. Our friend, being a marvelous free spirit, immediately began to butt into the conversation and after a short time we all were face-to-face. Jerry didn't recognize me at first and so my wife said to him: "Hey, Jerry, I really dug your speech." And, he in turn went into his little song-and-dance routine that signified that he was about to pick up a chick. So he said something like: "Yea, wow. Why don't we go to bed?" And she said: "No, but I did like that part about private property being pure s_." And Jerry got into it and said: "Yea, well property is s_ and after the revolution we will divide everything up. Like there won't be anything private. My shirt will be your shirt and my car will be your car. And it will be like one big commune."

And everybody standing around could dig on that because it sounded pretty far out—and the boys always dig the idea of sharing the girls—so Barbra went on. "That's a fantastic Indian head band you have on Jerry."

Retort: "Yea. It was given to me by a friend."

Barbra: "Why don't you give it to me?"

Jerry: "Huh?"

Barbra: "You said that private property was s_ so why won't you give me your head band."

Well, Rubin looked astonished and blurted out: "But it's my head band."

Yes, Jerry it is your head band.

And my head band is my hand band and that is called private property.

It was at about this juncture of disorientation that Barbra introduced me to Jerry. He really couldn't pull himself together. Here I was—the enemy incarnate—standing there just like the rest of the freaks and not brandishing my tape recorder or my nonexistent badge. It was too much. Rubin kept saying things like "Wow, there are a lot of people in Berkeley who want to kill you" and "You can't fool me with those sideburns" and to his heavy friend "Do you know who this is?" Finally, he just got up and said he had to split because there was something else he had to do—but earlier he had time to spare for Barbra.

It's that way with Rubin. I can only assume that Jerry does hate me. It's not like he knows me—although he writes as if he does. In fact, his little jab at me in *Do It!* is about as realistic as Yippiedom. For instance: I have never gone "skinnydipping with Fidel" and neither did anyone on our trip to Cuba in 1963. Romanticism has no place in spleen-letting. Next: I am hardly the only person to leave the New Left. The consistency of the New Left resembles a men's room. A lot of people seem to go into the Left and do their thing and then leave. I am hardly the virgin prince that Jerry would have me be.

Jerry would like to be an anarchist but he doesn't have the education. Jerry would like to be a revolutionary but the revolutionaries have moved on. Jerry would love to be an idol of the media but has reached the point of over-kill when he sees a camera. All we can hope is that someday, in someway, Jerry will find a way to *Do It!* without further inflicting himself upon us.

Of course, it's not only Rubin who understands power and the use of media. All the crazies utilize the so-called underground newspapers and periodicals in their efforts to proselytize the young and the disillusioned. I have always found it fascinating that in this age of revolt one of the first victims is semantics. The papers that are openly hawked on the streets of our major cities by youthful entrepreneurs are hardly "underground" in either form or distribution.

A corollary to this would be the so-called "free press" newspapers. The "free press" papers are a total misnomer. In the first instance, they are not "free" either in cost or in political content. The reader of the "free press" must pay for his paper, thereby denying the contention that the paper is "free." It should also be noted that while the "free press" concept exemplifies the purported libertine freedoms, in practice these papers argue for socialism and collectivism.

The "free press" and the crazies argue for a free sex and drug ethic that would lead the unwary to believe that if these two societal taboos were abolished man would find peace and freedom. This intellectually dishonest crutch has filtered throughout our society and we now can find mere children totally involved in the drug world.

No, drugs and sex alone will not free a person and they certainly will not free a society. I do not personally mind what another person does to himself or herself so long as he does not violate my rights, but I must state in all candor that the crazies are leading our children down a dead-end street.

Aldous Huxley wrote a brilliant novel entitled *Brave New World* in which the people were stoned most of the time on "soma." Today, we find our young more and more dependent upon various chemical substances in their desire to alter their sense of reality. Today the youth are using a myriad of chemical means to seek a false safety from the reality that surrounds them.

The crazies are naturally eager for the youth to become drug oriented if not indeed drug addicted. Drug addiction is often a psychological addiction more than a physical need or craving. These youths, once they are drug oriented, lose the perspective of reality and are willing to argue and insist that everyone get stoned. As if the very act itself would open magical doors, the crazies urge our youth to do anything once. To the political crazy there is no moral touch with reality.

Once the individual begins to submit his will to the crutch of drugs he is under the control of that crutch. The crazies argue that if sex and drugs were wide open in our society man would inherently be free. The leaders of the newspapers and organizations arguing this perspective know, however, that this is a lie.

Drugs lead into a state of slavery and not freedom. Once a large number of people become psychologically addicted to a drug (or drugs) they are openly admitting that they are incapable of functioning as free men. The people that are not taking drugs (or who have overcome the drug symbiosis) will naturally utilize the existing technology to deceive those who are under the influence of drugs.

In all candor, I must state that I do not know whether we can now control the drug problem. It is here and it is pervasive. The question is no longer one of legalizing or not legalizing marihuana but rather one of personal and individual commitment not to use drugs. Drugs are a part of our current culture and we as individuals must decide how to handle the problem.

It is natural that Hoffman and Rubin would love to see everyone stoned and making love in the parks. Not because it might be a beautiful act but rather because they would then know that the people had lost control and that they were ready for a strong "father figure" government to control them.

The key to the flawed nature of the crazies' position is that while they speak of total freedom they are always convinced that someone (usually unnamed but strongly resembling themselves) will have to be around to "help" the people. Rubin and Hoffman and company often urge their audiences to "trust them."

If indeed they have a program for the future, outside of some vague political nirvana, they rarely reveal this program. They ask the unwary to totally "trust them" in their cant and bravado. They say: do as I say and it will all turn out all right. Get stoned, read some Mao, read the "Free Press," live in a commune and you will find the light.

The crazy ethic calls on you to think of all police as "pigs" and not differentiate between a good and a bad policeman. The crazy ethic claims that violence is inherently good and that something valid is accomplished by destroying bank windows, cars, or people who happen to be on-the-other-side politically. Jack Anderson reported in the July 28, 1970, issue of the Washington Post that:

> "The FBI has learned from undercover sources that a black extremist group, which calls itself the True Black Family, requires recruits to bring in two white ears as the grisly price of membership.
>
> "The FBI has received a report that at least one victim, a 16-year-old white hitchhiker in Michigan, was slain by True Black Family believers. The body was found with no ears."

That is how crazy things have now gotten in this nation. It is not black people that are crazy but a minority of all races that seek to demand their own truth and justice at the expense of other individuals.

The crazies and the Weatherpeople have also been primarily responsible for the continuing futile process of confrontation politics in this nation. The crazies are masters at creating cases in which a confrontation between the police and themselves will culminate in violence—not only to both of these parties, but also to innocent bystanders.

Confrontation is designed to force the police into action against a group of demonstrators in order to place the police in the worst possible media spotlight. With this in mind the crazies are out to create disruption and confrontation wherever possible.

An interaction process also takes place in the confrontation syndrome, and this process is too often missed or ignored by the crazies. As the confrontation tactic increases, and more and more physical and psychic damage is done to the community at large, the process of repression also begins to grow. The problem with repression is that it tends to grow geometrically. There is good reason to believe that as people tire of the excesses of the crazies and their cohorts that they will cheer on the tactics of the government designed to counter the crazies in the short run—but certain to limit freedom in the long run.

The interaction between confrontation and repression has not been studied or detailed enough in this nation. Unfortunately, I fear that our evidence of this interaction may be provided empirically.

The crazies also seem to have no knowledge or interest in the lessons of history. If indeed, by some bizzare happenstance, the left-wing revolution came to fruition in this nation the crazies would be among the first to literally find themselves in the "country of the damned." Socialist revolutions have historically been most apt at taking care of the local crazies and outspoken anarchists. But, of course, the Rubins and Hoffmans hope that "come the revolution" they will be given their rightful place in the hierarchy.

Ultimately, however, the crazies likely will destroy themselves. They deny that philosophy and history have any role in reality. Instead, the crazies demand action. The problem they now face is that the violence they have fostered is returning to devour them.

THE TROTSKYITES 10

TIMES change, especially with the little Lenins of this country. A book I wrote in 1966, *The New Left*, dealt with the American Trotskyite movement in a chapter entitled "The Outsiders." The Trots are now the insiders and as such are one of the most potent forces in the history of American radicalism.

Leading the forces of the Trotskyite Fourth International in the United States is the Socialist Workers Party (SWP), founded in 1938 by James P. Cannon. (He had been booted out of the Communist Party on charges of opposing the Stalinist horrors in favor of those perpetrated by Lenin's old sidekick, Leon Trotsky.)

SWP membership stands at about 1000. That figure may be unimpressive but recent results in terms of "radicalizing the masses" have been nothing less than spectacular.

The SWP's dirty work is handled by its youth affiliate, the Young Socialist Alliance. The YSA egg was hatched by SWP in 1960.

In terms of numerical membership the YSA fares little better than its adult counterpart. The membership figure quoted at the YSA's 1970 national convention was 1224.

The YSA carries out SWP dictates through its "locals" scattered around the country. Locals vary in membership from a required minimum of five to a high of 200 members in New York City.

Hot issues with which the YSA concerns itself are fairly typical for a modern day New Left group: The war in Vietnam (Out Now!—immediate withdrawal); racial issues (support black nationalism); Arabs vs. Israelis (the Israelis are Zionist aggressors); Chicano liberation (Right on!); and finally women's liberation.

In terms of SWP/YSA membership, the Republic is facing 2000 Trotskyites at most (the SWP/YSA membership overlaps in certain locales). But here's the key to Trotskyite success: They control—outright—both the Student Mobilization Committee To End the War In Vietnam (SMC) *and* the National Peace Action Coalition (NPAC).

SMC and NPAC illustrate the united front concept: Attract as many organizations and individuals as possible and get them to push your line. This concept works. The Communist Party proved it in the 1930's and the Trots are proving it in the 1970's.

Four factors have led to the overwhelming success of Trotskyite efforts to control massive united front groups such as SMC and NPAC:

1.) The Young Socialist Alliance has been able to maintain the pretense of being a relatively independent organization. Most YSA members and officers (on the local level) are not members of the Socialist Workers Party. The SWP line is the gospel truth for the YSA, but at least the SWP is not overbearing with its presence.

2.) YSA'ers come off looking like the "young socialists" they claim to be, especially when compared to the old "youth" of other radical organizations. Twenty-five is the age at which YSA'ers are expected to start packing for Socialist Workers Party graduate school.

3.) The Young Socialist Alliance has learned that the

best way to involve hundreds of thousands of sheep is to pick a single issue around which most leftists can agree. At present, it's the demand for an immediate end to U.S. involvement in Southeast Asia. Other radical groups like to confuse the issue by dragging in questions of racism, welfare and the like. Not all leftists agree on the solutions to these problems, but all leftists agree that U.S. presence in Vietnam is a very bad thing.

4.) The break-up of Students For a Democratic Society (SDS) has benefited the YSA immeasurably. A few former SDS'ers actually joined the Young Socialist Alliance. One local SDS chapter in Kansas, for example, voted to become a YSA local. More important, however, are those thousands of SDS'ers who suddenly found themselves without a home. They had to go somewhere. Many of them selected the YSA-controlled "Student Mobe."

The rise of the Young Socialist Alliance to the leading spot on the American left is directly related to its control of the Student Mobilization Committee.

During the summer of 1968 the YSA brazenly challenged Communist Party control of the Student Mobe. Running the Student Mobe show at that time were Linda Morse (an "independent" who knew the CP line and liked to follow it), Gwen Patton, Clark Lobenstine, Phyllis Kalb (a CP member at Brooklyn College), and Leslie Cagan (wife of Steve Cagan; both husband and wife received their radical education through the DuBois Club at Indiana University). Of the five SMC coordinators named above, the CP could count on three.

This would have been a very happy situation for the Communist Party were it not for the fact that Kipp Dawson and Syd Stapleton, both YSA members, were working in the Student Mobe national office and interfering with Communist Party control of the organization at every available opportunity.

The CP-YSA feud reached the boiling point, and after much internal warfare, the Student Mobe ended up controlled by the Trotskyite SWP and YSA.

This was the start of the Trotskyite rise to power within the American left. The Trots worked hard to solidify their ill-gotten gains. Out went the confusing issues of draft resistance and racism. In came the single issue of "U.S. Out of Vietnam Now!"

The Student Mobilization Committee grew in strength because there was now a central theme around which all leftists could gather.

YSA locals were ordered to give top priority to building Student Mobe chapters in their localities. Local independent anti-war groups were invaded by the Young Socialist Alliance and suddenly found themselves voting to affiliate with the Student Mobilization Committee.

YSA members worked to fill local SMC leadership slots with their own members, or at least persons known to be good buddies with local Trotskyite elements. An early illustration can be found at one of the country's largest universities. The local Student Mobe chairman was a YSA member; so was the entire executive committee with the exception of two members, one of whom was a former YSA member.

The only known cases in which the Young Socialist Alliance has lost control of local Student Mobe chapters are at Columbia University where it is controlled by the International Socialists, and at Temple University in Philadelphia. The latter case is noteworthy only because of its hilarity. During one recent summer, when many of the Trotskyite faithful were out of town, the Young Workers Liberation League (the Communist Party youth group) moved in and took over the Temple Student Mobe. Upon their return in September, however, the Trots discovered what had happened and proceeded to regain control.

With the Student Mobilization Committee firmly under YSA control, a series of local and national demonstrations was called. The national actions, centered in Washington and San Francisco, were generally a success. Student Mobe-sponsored *local* demonstrations, however, bordered on dismal failures. After all, it's much more exciting to parade around Washington and shout obscenities there than at the local town square.

Not satisfied with merely controlling the anti-war element within the academe, the SWP/YSA strategists began looking for ways to involve unions, GI's, veterans, women's groups, church groups and the like. The result was the formation of the National Peace Action Coalition, founded in July of 1970.

A call was issued for anti-war activists to report to Cleveland's Cuyahoga Community College. Hosted by the

Cleveland Area Peace Action Coalition (a local Trotskyite front), the conference was designed to create an anti-war umbrella group under which all sorts of diverse organizations could gather and push the single demand of an immediate end to U.S. involvement in Southeast Asia. The conference was also designed to map future anti-war activity.

The result of the call was an outpouring of about 1000 Student Mobe members, 300 Progressive Labor Party shock troops determined to disrupt the conference, a smattering of far-out types from the Workers League, International Socialists and Spartacist League, plus a few Communist Party bigwigs from New York who went to view the latest Trotskyite undertaking.

Things went quite smoothly for the Trotskyites. There was no doubt that they had the numerical strength to call the shots. So solid was their control of the conference that they even tolerated Progressive Labor's outrageous deportment.

At one point during the screaming from Progressive Labor's section of the convention floor, Fred Halstead, a portly SWP'er from New York, marched on stage to give orders to the conference chairman. PL's storm troopers, fists raised in a show of Maoist solidarity, began shouting "Halstead Off, Halstead Off!" Halstead was so sure of Trotskyite control that he jokingly joined the PL cheerleaders.

Eventually the Progressive Labor rooting section yelled itself hoarse and the Trotskyites proceeded to ram through their program.

The National Peace Action Coalition was formed. It would be run—ostensibly—by five coordinators: Jerry Gordon (a Socialist Workers Party collaborator heading the Cleveland Area Peace Action Coalition), Jim Lafferty of Detroit (no enemy of the SWP/YSA), Don Gurewitz of the SWP and Student Mobe, John T. Williams (Vice President of the Los Angeles Teamsters), and Ruth Gage-Colby (of Women's International League For Peace and Freedom). In reality NPAC is run by only three of the above: Gordon, Lafferty and Gurewitz. John T. Williams and Ruth Gage-Colby are for show purposes only. With the line-up of Gordon, Lafferty and Gurewitz, the Trotskyites were sitting pretty.

(A slight alteration in the NPAC leadership roster was made in July, 1971. Debby Bustin, an officer of the Student Mobe and member of the YSA, was named to replace Don Gurewitz as an NPAC coordinator.)

Programmatically, the Trotskyites took the successful Student Mobe position of single issue mass action and saw to it that NPAC adopted the same line.

The Trotskyite anti-war united front was now complete. Students could rally around the Student Mobe. Non-students and, more importantly, entire organizations could work with NPAC.

Of the two groups, the National Peace Action Coalition is of greater significance when it comes to mobilizing the angry masses. Since it is not burdened by the label of a student organization, as is the Student Mobilization Committee, NPAC can muster the support of countless groups, individuals and politicians. Student Mobe provides the muscle and does the dirty work; NPAC serves to legitimize that dirty work.

NPAC-sponsored actions have been tremendously successful on the national level. A demonstration on April 24, 1971 mobilized upwards of 250,000 of the gullible.

To tally the Trotskyite scorecard: The Socialist Workers Party runs the Young Socialist Alliance. The YSA in turn controls the Student Mobilization Committee. The Student Mobe, under the guiding hand of YSA, is what makes NPAC tick. The result of all this intrigue is a dangerously potent force.

The SWP/YSA combination is not alone in claiming to be the only true Trotskyite element in the country. The Workers League and the Spartacist League are both fond of claiming to know the only true path to revolution a la Trotsky. Both are SWP/YSA splinter groups and both are woefully small and generally impotent.

The Workers League, centered around New York City, is headed by Tim Wohlforth. Wohlforth has been relatively silent in recent years, preferring to leave a great deal of the public speaking to Pat Connelly, a WL member at The City College of New York. Given the slightest provocation, Miss Connelly will deliver a ten minute harangue in which she repeats everything the Workers League has ever written, thought or said.

Aside from publishing its *Bulletin* and making proposals at SMC and NPAC conventions (which are invariably defeated) the Workers League does little else.

WL maintains that the only true road to revolution in this country is the creation of a "labor party" through which the toiling masses of Pittsburgh and other industrial centers will lead students in creating the dictatorship of the proletariat.

Much Workers League energy is given to attacking the SWP/YSA. Without the larger Trotskyite groups to criticize, the Workers League would likely fold in rapid fashion.

Even less can be said for the Spartacist League. Headed by Jim Robertson, a rather amiable fellow, Spartacist publishes a totally absurd periodical titled *Spartacist*. While the Workers League *Bulletin* is oriented toward taking pot shots at the SWP/YSA, *Spartacist* gives equal time to both the SWP/YSA and Progressive Labor.

Spartacist, too, makes appearances at Student Mobe and NPAC gatherings, puts forth its proposals, suffers ignominious defeat, and goes home to bemoan its fate in the next issue of *Spartacist*.

At the July, 1971, convention of the National Peace Action Coalition, Spartacist showed its taste for violence by teaming up with Progressive Labor in disrupting the convention and then physically attacking New York City police.

We turn now to the real outsiders—the lonely and (deservedly) forgotten of the Young Workers Liberation League. The YWLL is controlled by the Communist Party. Its purpose is primarily that of providing the CP with badly needed young recruits.

In the past ten years the CP has had four different youth groups: Advance, Provisional Youth Organizing Committee, W.E.B. DuBois Clubs, and now the YWLL. The first three organizations failed miserably and the YWLL is apparently following the trend established by its predecessors.

Part of the Communist Party problem with youth stems from the fact that the Party has never been able to decide whether a youth group should be geared toward working class young people or students. Presumably the CP hopes to reach a happy medium with the YWLL which has sections for working youth as well as students.

As might be expected, the industrial branches of the YWLL are faring badly due largely to the fact that young people who work for a living tend to have a lot more on the ball than their student counterparts. A young person facing the financial realities of supporting a family is simply too concerned with improving his lot to be taken in by the revolutionary fantasies of the Young Workers Liberation League.

To illustrate the lack of workers in the Young Workers Liberation League, recent testimony before the House Internal Security Committee brought to light an amusing story. The House Committee "surfaced" one of its YWLL infiltrators, a student at John Jay College in New York City, who reported telling the YWLL that he was employed as a "laundry worker." The YWLL was so overjoyed at the prospect of recruiting a real live worker that it immediately gave the committee infiltrator a top leadership slot in the Lower East Side YWLL.

The YWLL came upon the American radical scene in 1970. Here is the background: In 1968, with the DuBois Clubs suffering from rigor mortis, the Communist Party sprung into action and decided to form YWLL. Robert Heisler and a few other young CP'ers from New York were sent on tours of CP clubs to whip up enthusiasm for the new group. Many of the young Communist Party members, having already surpassed the old CP heavies in terms of stodginess, balked at the idea of a new organization. Nostalgia was the reason. Many of the young CP'ers had been recruited through the DuBois Clubs and simply could not bear the thought of having to do away with the DuBois Clubs.

Ultimately, of course, the CP heavies in New York had their way and launched the YWLL at a Chicago founding conference held in February, 1970. Some 400 of the faithful attended—most of them already in the Communist Party. In typical CP fashion, the conference was by invitation only. And to this day the CP wonders why its YWLL has such a small following.

The Young Workers Liberation League differs little from the old DuBois Clubs. Indeed the roster of YWLL officers is strikingly similar to that of the DuBois Clubs: Jarvis Tyner, chairman; Mike Zagarell, education director; Rocque Ristorucci, publications director; Judy Edelman, director of labor; and Barry Cohen, organizational secretary.

YWLL membership is less than one thousand, many of whom are members of the Party. Nonetheless the YWLL foresees bigger and better things. Jarvis Tyner has set a goal of 50,000 YWLL members. That ridiculous figure is probably due to the fact that Jarvis was recently struck in the head with the collected works of Gus Hall. (During the DuBois Club days, CP boss Hall personally intervened and set a membership goal of 50,000.) It is unlikely that the YWLL membership figure will go much higher than 1000.

The YWLL is hampered by two major factors:

1.) It is widely recognized among leftists as a Communist Party youth group. Young people on the left have the CP marked for exactly what it is: A stodgy, old-line radical outfit which has steadfastly refused to adjust to the New Left. The Communist Party label will lead to the YWLL's inevitable death.

2.) The YWLL and its parent organization have refused to take lessons from the Trotskyites when it comes to organizing masses of people. The Trots employ the single issue of immediate withdrawal of U.S. forces from Vietnam. The YWLL takes a more conservative approach by calling for the U.S. to set a date for withdrawal. The YWLL then drags in the issues of welfare, racism, etc. The result, of course, is inability to find masses of people who can agree on solutions to these problems.

The Young Workers Liberation League simply is not and never will be a significant force within the American left. As with past CP youth groups, the Party will milk the YWLL for as many recruits as possible and then proceed to ditch the organization.

WHATEVER HAPPENED TO THE EARLY NEW LEFT ? 11

THE New Left is polymorphic. It has divided and subdivided to the point where no rational human observer can talk about *the* New Left. If there ever was a monolithic New Left it certainly no longer exists. More importantly, however, is the fact that there is no longer such a thing as a "new"left operating in the United States. What passes for "New" Leftist thought in this country is seldom more than traditional repressive Communist ideology foisted on young people via the "youth" groups of old line Communist organizations. Once you cut through the revolutionary rhetoric of the myriad of student "new" Left sects you discover a wobbling house of cards. The "new" Left is a child's temper tantrum computerized into inter-state revolution. The "new" Left is as philosophically progressive as Joe Stalin and as politically cohesive as three power-hungry Trotskyites. The "new" Left is as concerned with human rights as the Ku Klux Klan and as devoted to civil liberties as Mao.

143

Liberal pundits and collectivist politicians have lauded the "new" Left and praised the "concern" of its self-appointed leaders. The national publicity machine has led many to assume that a "new" Left actually exists. Many people are prone to praise the "new" Left while only occasionally disassociating the revolutionaries from the general membership. It's gotten to the point where on many campuses every time you try to talk about the "new" Left some Wally Whizbang jumps up and claims immunity from your description because although he claims membership in the broad category he demands exclusion from the specific definition. These monologues usually take this form: "Listen, Luce, what you say about the SDS at Columbia may be true, but here at Snail's Pace University we are not like that. To place the New Left in a category is unfair and absurd."

At some schools I have visited the local "new" Left outfits were adamant in denying any relationship with their revolutionary brothers and sisters at other universities. The mass media and the gobbledygook politicians often play on this separatist concept by accepting the "new" Left's societal criticisms while smugly renouncing the violence of the extremist elements in the movement.

One of the immediate problems in playing an exclusionist game with the "new" Left is that it soon leads to intellectual relativism. Of course, the admitted "new" Leftists in Alabama are going to talk another game from those in San Francisco, but this is a question of tactics and not one of politics.

The term "new" Left is a creation of the mass media and today has no relationship to the product under discussion. The word "new" implies originality, a novel approach. It is true that when SDS (who along with the now defunct SNCC organization were the original "new" Left) was founded, it did herald a break with some of the philosophical and political laws of the left-wing. Today, however, the stance of SDS and collateral groups is hardly "new" in any sense except as a publicity image.

The concept of a "new" Left also implies that the movement is seeking answers to political questions in a context different from the "old" Left. This further implies some basic philosophical differences between the elder and younger movements. The term "new" Left also conjures up the impression that the "old" Left (in this case pragmatically meaning the Communist Party of the United States) is politically and philosophically out-of-step with the "new" Left. It also means that the "new" Left is independent from the confines of an older Marxist–Leninist approach to the strategy and tactics of today's battles.

Originally, SDS did exclude Communists from its membership. Today, that exclusionist policy has changed to inclusion and the present ruling figures of the SDS proudly proclaim their communism (using the tactic of a small "c" to exclude themselves from an existing Communist Party and create additional confusion).

A letter from the SDS National Office dated June 23, 1969, and addressed to the membership states that "We must be clear that we will never tolerate anti-communism in our movement." This letter was signed by the top five leaders of SDS including Mark Rudd, the National Secretary.

For all intents, the "new" Left is merely some distorted mirror image of the "old" Left. The difference that exists between the youthful revolutionaries and their parent ideologues is generational rather than philosophical.

The "new" Left is part and parcel of the Marxist-Leninist philosophy that is determined to destroy capitalism and establish totalitarianism. In the United States, the "new" Left has taken up the mantle of revolutionary Communism in its rhetoric and tactical approach to destroying the "system" (read capitalism).

The Left is not stupid. Tactics necessitate the need to play various "roles" at specific times and in specific circumstances. This is why a "new" leftist will speak softly in Alabama and will raise the red flag at Stanford. Tactics also dictate the semantic break used to attack the "old and worn out" rhetoric and practices of the CPUSA.

Tactics therefore demand that the "new" Left disavow the "old" Left—much as "new energized Smack" the dish-washing miracle disavows the old-fashioned washboard Smack. Utilizing the precepts of the market-place (which the left-wing would

joyously destroy) the "new" Left has simply reworked its
public image in order to sell its shoddy political line to young
people and to confuse those older people more interested in
style than in content.

I am the first to admit that initially the "new" Left seemed
willing to espouse a political line that denied the inevitability of
Marx's laws of politics. Many early recruits to the "new" Left
felt that it was a break with the past and that the "newness"
would also develop into a philosophical schism with the socialist
scheme. This hope has been consistently smashed to bits since
1965. Anyone who today still harbors the belief that the "new"
Left is operating out of a separate set of dogma from the "old"
Left has been deluded by reading and believing political
rhetoric.

The majority of young people affiliated with the "new" Left
are idealists seeking some solution to the often grotesque
problems facing this nation. Youth usually seeks immediate
changes for obvious problems. The Left has always held out
immediate and total change as the solution for political, social
and economic problems. The Left says: if you are distressed
with conditions then join us and we will not simply change
things but deliver a pie in the sky. The Left guarantees (with the
satisfaction of most used car dealers) an end of all problems and
a near immediate heaven on earth policy. In the United States
we are told by the spokesmen of revolution that this change will
come through an "American revolution." It will not be like any
other revolution (Chinese, Cuban, Russian, etc.), but will be
endemic to this nation. With that refusal to read or understand
history that is the near-monopoly of idealistic youth, many
students fall for the line. The membership is often prone to
actually despise the pragmatic conditions of those who
unfortunately have to live under Communism and they deny
that "their revolution" would culminate in such a horror.
History, however, shows that the same revolutionary lie has
been spread by the Left throughout the world—"this revolution
will be truly unique." And, of course, each revolution is unique.
Still, the record shows that once the revolution has succeeded,
socialist collectivism replaces the status quo and merely creates

a new power structure determined to impose its dictates (in the name of "freedom") over the free will of the people.

The socialism of a Tom Hayden or Mark Rudd is as stultifying to the individual as that espoused by Gus Hall, Eldridge Cleaver or Mao Tse-Tung. How many times must the flowery promises of peace and beauty be turned into laws of tyranny and state control before people will consider logic above emotion.

The student revolutionaries are playing games with other people's minds. Stephen Spender has written in *The Year of the Young Rebels* that the "students are convinced that their revolution will not be like any other. In Paris or Berlin they will explain to you that the 'bases' will be democratic, that there will be no leaders, that the 'structures' will be different. They will cite Castro and Che and Mao to show that the revolution can be 'permanent' and continue evolving under leaders who are prepared to discuss their policies with people they meet in the street. If one mentions the French Revolution began with committees planning Utopias, orations, turbulent figures voicing their wish for anonymity, they reply that they are an unprecedented generation."

The New Left talks a good line, but their politics are merely a stage set for their actual nature. The "new" Left is opposed to the draft only because they hate the war in Vietnam and not because they are opposed to involuntary servitude. The "new" Left believes in free speech for themselves but not for their opponents or detractors. The "new" Left espouses violence and acts as if they were a hippie Red Guard movement. The "new" Left speaks of problems but offers no obvious solutions.

Slogans are not solutions. The "new" Left is intelligent enough to realize that the solutions it has for this society are not going to be accepted by students, workers or voters. If the "new" Left told the truth about its actual goals (anywhere except in its internal documents) it would turn off most potential members. So the "new" Left organizes and recruits around vague generalities.

The final SDS national convention should provide ample evidence to anyone interested that the "new" Left has finally dropped its "newness." As I mentioned earlier the SDS convention broke apart once it became obvious that the Progressive Labor Party (overt Chinese Communist types) was on the threshold of physically taking over SDS. The minority faction at the convention (represented by the national office staff of SDS) walked out of the Convention and then summarily dismissed the PL group from the organization.

Following the expulsion, the SDS office staff proclaimed itself to be the "only true and factual SDS." The PL people cried sham, but to no avail. Progressive Labor now finds itself outside the mainstream of "new" Left strategy for revolution.

It would be a mistake, however, to assume that the ouster of Progressive Labor signaled a defeat for Marxism-Leninism among the "new" Left. The mass media played up the split because it would appear to the uninitiated that the hard-core Communists had been purged from SDS and that only rational spokesmen for change remained. In reality, the purge of PL does not signal any serious lessening of the revolutionary tenor of the "new" Left.

Once Progressive Labor was driven out of SDS, the apologists for the purge began to argue that it was a philosophical question rather than a power play.

An early leader of SDS, Carl Davidson, took to the pages of the left-wing newsweekly *Guardian* to explain the purge as follows:

> " 'The principal contradiction in the world today is that between U.S. imperialism and the nations it oppresses. The sharpest blows against oppressed peoples of Asia, Africa, Latin America and within the U.S.'
>
> —from the five principles of SDS unity proposed by the revolutionary youth movement faction at the SDS convention.
>
> " 'The principal contradiction in the world today is between U.S. imperialism and Soviet revisionism on the one hand, and the world's oppressed worker-peasant masses on the other.' "
>
> —from a speech by Jeff Gordon of the Progressive Labor Party during the SDS convention:

"The theoretical basis for the expulsion of the Progressive Labor Party from SDS has its roots in the differences between the statements above. Some may think it a small matter or a technical point; it is not. For what a revolutionary movement holds to be the 'principal contradiction in the world today' determines not only the direction and content of its theoretical work, but shapes all aspects of its program, organization and practical activity. It determines how one assesses and relates to revolutionary struggles, both international and local.

"This became clear in the split which developed in SDS chapters over the past year—PL/worker-student alliance caucuses and the revolutionary youth movement groups were diametrically opposed on almost every aspect of political activity.

"The theoretical differences between the two groups center on what Marxists have called 'the national question.' The issue is the relation between nationalism and national movements, and the international working-class revolutionary movement for socialism."

Later on in the same article, Davidson states quite concisely that the "principle at stake is socialist internationalism." He then tells his readers that Progressive Labor is at fault because it "ignores most of the experience of the international socialist movement from Marx through Mao."

The issue developed by Davidson (and argued at the SDS convention by various left-wing sects) is one of internal Marxist-Leninist strategy and tactics, and not one of a new and vital approach to change through peaceful means. I have read the documents from the SDS convention and each side argued the "national question" from the basis of how many quotes from Stalin, Mao and Lin Piao could be garnered to reinforce its position.

The point here is not to take sides within the left-wing discussion of the accuracy of Stalin's analysis in his *Marxism and the National Question* published in 1913. The fact that the battle could even rage within the "new" Left is revealing. Shades of Trotsky and De Leon. Even an intellectual eunuch should be able to see that the "new" Left is only split over the correct analysis to be employed to destroy capitalism. If this is a "new" quest for truth then so is *Das Capital.*

Splits and internal fratricide are not new to the socialistic political camp. Historically, the Left has been internally divided over how best to impose socialism over the world. The Bolshevik-Menshevik battle; the Stalin-Trotsky split; the Russian-Chinese controversy; the Cuban-Russian debate over the "means" to be used in South America all reflect the constant struggle existing among Marxist-Leninist parties determined to destroy capitalism and impose socialism.

Even after the SDS convention some people argue there are a significant number of young "new" Leftists who are really libertarians. These people argue that to attack the "new" Left as a Marxist-Leninist prototype is to ignore the aspirations and hopes of this minority. My purpose is not to ignore those few young people who were misguided into believing that SDS was intrinsically libertarian, but to insist that libertarians have better sense than to fall for socialism or collectivism in whatever guise it presents itself. It should not be necessary for me to have to prove the "new" Left is left-wing and therefore collectivist by the very nature of its existence, but rather for its devotees to prove the opposite. Of course, behind the revolutionary rhetoric you find not libertarianism but collectivism.

It is not fashionable to call the "new" Left collectivist or totalitarian. To refer to the young revolutionaries as Marxist-Leninists and/or Communists may smack some of "McCarthyism" but the truth is hard to hide. The "new" Left only exists in the minds of those people who refuse to accept the reality of existing situations. The Left is a reality in this country and it is past time we continued to play the game (with the rules imposed by Liberal apologists and their left-wing allies) that a "new" Left somehow is a different entity from the "old" Left.

WHAT IS TO BE DONE ? **12**

AND now we reach the last chapter of the book. Some of my left-wing detractors would have you believe that I sit here enveloped in the flag with a hard hat on my head. Because I am opposed to collectivism and communism, I am often pictured as an arm of the establishment. Tom Hayden speaking at the University of Idaho called me a "psychedelic FBI agent" and the Los Angeles Black Panthers refer to me as the "hippy honky." Jerry Rubin and the devotees of Progressive Labor are less laudatory. My leftist detractors also credit me with formulating ultimate solutions to our societal problems. The reality of the matter was captured some time ago by Hadrian: "For some years now people have credited me with strange insights, and with knowledge of divine secrets. But they are mistaken; I have no such power."

Everywhere I go, the hard-core leftist types are convinced that I have a microphone in my sideburns and a subpoena in my

151

pocket. As I wrote this chapter, I put my wife and child on an airplane for California and asked a young man beside her to please be so kind as to assist her with a parcel or two. He agreed, and later I was amazed to learn that he lectured Barbra about how I was an "FBI agent" and other such irrationalities. This young traveler was a radical at the University of California at San Diego and had apparently identified me from the stories his compatriots tell of us breakaways.

No, I am not now nor have I ever been an agent for this or any government. I have never been anything other than a man trying to make some sense out of the panoplay of political schizophrenia that daily surrounds us. I was once a communist but like the myriad of people before and after me, I have left "the faith" and am again an individual, unaligned and unaffiliated with any of the existing political parties. I went through an experience and I learned something from it. For that alone I am thankful.

There was no big jump for me. I was not on the ultra-left one day and on the ultra-right the next day. I was a communist for a short period of time. Actually, the Trotskyites have always been right in their characterization of me as a "bourgeois radical." I was a poor communist and I am ever grateful to the ineptitude of Progressive Labor for having given me too much of an organizational push too fast. I will only note that my political proclivities today are quite similar to those I held prior to becoming involved in the morass of Marxist-Leninist theology. I have made no jump from extreme to extreme. I made a horrid mistake and I am today attempting to rectify that mistake by opposing all collectivist and totalitarian doctrines.

I am not a "professional ex-communist." My purpose in life is not to live by recounting my past sins. I would much rather be known as a bad poet than as merely an ex-communist. Or, for that matter, I would rather be known for something positive than for something "anti".

The purpose of this book, however, is not to subject the reader to a course in the Luce theory of political utopias. The purpose of this book is to give you some insight into the formation and ultimate intellectual rape of the organized New Left. The purpose of this book is hopefully to also encourage a few people to begin to question the now popular mores of self-indulgent children simply demanding that everyone "do it."

To coin a Chairman Maoism, what we need to do in this country is, "dare to struggle, dare to win."

I cannot help but sense an inherent refusal to admit the inner truth of this Maoist maxim. I intuit that we as a people have stopped struggling because we no longer know what we dare to win. I am most explicitly not talking about some messianic complex desirous of implementing the American flag in every capital of this galaxy.

The struggle of which I write is the eternal struggle of man to live in peace among other men determined to subject him to their own particular will. Most politics (except on the "practical" level) are concerned with improving the lot of man. No one could openly argue to "disimprove" the level of mankind. Some seek this better life through the collectivist ideologies of communism, socialism or fascism. Others seek the better life through the process of the free market and individual freedom. This is not meant to imply a closed circuit, as the possible variations on the scheme are legend.

In the early 1960's the young New Leftists looked at society and decided it needed changing. The instinctive impulse was good. Who could seriously agree with the good Dr. Pangloss that this is "the best of all possible worlds"?

The virginal New Left honestly criticized our society, but it managed to come up with a false solution. A revolution aimed at overthrowing one government and then superimposing another structure modelled on "1984" is anti-intellectual, anti-life and anti-libertarian. Equally absurd is the "crazy" concept that once this government is destroyed man will live in instinctual, perfect harmony through the osmosis of drugs, free sex and some yet unexplained free spirit.

The "ends justify the means" syndrome doesn't even apply to the "crazies" because once our specific, pragmatic, objective, real government and constitution is revolutionized out of existence, they will be the first to suffer the unveiled fist of the new collectivist government. Have the pragmatics of Cuba, China, the Soviet Union, Czechoslovakia, Poland, *ad infinitum* taught us nothing?

153

One vital suicidal instinct functioning within the broad New Left was its refusal to organize a viable non-communist movement. The communists, on the other hand, utilized their historical perspectives and their studied ability to "capture organizations in order to make them run more smoothly" to destroy the initiative and bravado of the early New Leftists. Today, with the exception of a few of the early founders of the New Left who have moved on to non-party radical affiliations, the whole of the movement is confined in the Jekyll-Hyde world of Maoism/Yippiedom.

If the New Left is passe, we are left with a real struggle pitting individualism against the dragons of collectivism and governmental bureaucracy.

But if indeed we have seen through the myth of beneficent, paternalistic government then we must also realize that violence will only lead us to disaster. The totalitarian forces are prepared to move whenever they feel truly threatened. The communists in our midst coupled with the politically drugged "crazies" are advancing their own Armageddon. The unfortunate fact is that few people are attempting to come up with creative counter-proposals to the political terrorism now so rampant in this nation. A Treasury official recently told a Senate investigating committee that "4,330 bombings in the last 15½ months have left more than 40 persons dead and 384 injured and caused more than $22 million in property damage."

The intensifying level of violence in this nation (between whites and blacks, children and parents, the state apparatus and the people, and people and people) is past the discussion point. The violence that is beginning to engulf us is similar to the marijuana that presently beclouds much of our youth. In both cases the first step is admitting that a problem exists and that we are no longer afraid to take individual action. Many sophomoric leftists are now arguing the proposition that certain crimes committed in this society are not really crimes at all but political acts disguised as murder, arson or bombing.

The government conducted one of its top-level show-case investigations into "campus unrest" in 1970. An expected list of authorities appeared before the blue ribbon panel and most argued that indeed the government had become unresponsive to the young. But one witness split the air. David Keene, national chairman of Young Americans for Freedom, told the commission a number of facts it possibly did not want to hear. Among other things, David noted that: "This tendency to justify violence by pointing to policies one disagrees with symbolizes more than anything else the rejection of the democratic process by a significant number of students on the Left. They, and many who listen to them, seem to have developed an esentially Latin American conception of what the democratic process is all about. They think democracy is fine so long as it works, which of course means so long as the policies they favor are adopted, but reject it when they don't like the results."

The struggle for free speech is double edged. Man must have the right to criticize his government, but he must also have the right to criticize those who criticize the state and perhaps him. The horror show presently being perpetrated by the left-wing amalgam works under the assumption they possess total truth.

Three years ago, I debated a young SDS protagonist who also happened to be the student body president at Washington University in St. Louis. This young man was determined on the issue of Vietnam. He argued well and had his facts correct. Still, he argued that we needed more participatory democracy in this nation. I agreed, and attempted to provoke him into a discussion of the merits of "participatory democracy" by asking him if we could agree on a hypothetical study.

In its ultimate form "participatory democracy" would mean that each individual would directly cast his "ballot" on each important issue facing the nation. A massive town meeting approach to politics. In this case, let us assume that the city of St. Louis is to vote on whether or not we shall remain in Vietnam (at that time this was an issue). After the citizenry has been thoroughly deluged with all phases of the arguments both for and against the question they will vote. We will assume that they have had the ability to see all of the data available and have made rational judgements based upon this input.

Now, they vote. The vote produces a majority "in favor" of our remaining in Southeast Asia (remember this is hypothetical). What do you do?

The young man looked at me and with all sincerity said: "That's easy. They would all be wrong." Maybe indeed they would "all be wrong", but the essence of the young man's participatory democracy concept was rooted in the democratic essence of abiding by the vote.

But the Left no longer will abide by the vote. It is now obvious that the left-wing has utter contempt for the democratic process. For that percentage of the population that relates to the Hoffman, Rubin, Eldridge Cleaver, Herbert Marcuse confederation, the mental barricades are already erected.

For truly freedom-loving Americans, there are alternatives. And a basic questioning of the duties of government is a start. As the great American libertarian sage Frank Chodorov has written: "One indication of how far the integration has gone is the disappearance of any discussion of the State *qua* State—a discussion that engaged the best minds of the eighteenth and nineteenth centuries. The inadequacies of a particular regime, or its personnel, are under constant attack, but there is no faultfinding with the institution itself. The State is all right, by common agreement, and it would work perfectly if the 'right' people were at the helm . . . The idea that this power apparatus is indeed the enemy of Society, that the interests of these institutions are in opposition is simply unthinkable. If it is brought up, it is dismissed as 'old fashioned,' which it is; until the modern era, it was an axiom that the State bears constant watching, the pernicious proclivities are built into it."

I am inclined to the view that while we must defend our nation from collectivism and totalitarianism, whether from within or without, we must also confront the basic problem inherent within an ever increasing governmental bureaucracy and control of our everyday lives.

The one accomplishment that I can credit the New Left with is the current near hysteria that it has generated in this nation and the potential for a nationwide governmental crackdown on all dissent in this nation. When governmental bureaucrats can seriously consider the proposal of a self-proclaimed psychiatrist from New York that all six-year-old children in the nation should be given tests in order to show if they exhibit "anti-social behavior" and the rejects are to be incarcerated in "rehabilitation camps" until they readjust, then the nation is indeed in serious trouble.

In those moments of despair when I sense a total confrontation between the evils of the state and of the left-wing, I recall the words of Jose Ortega y Gasset who said: "This is the gravest danger that today threatens civilization: State intervention, the absorption of all spontaneous social effort by the State; that is to say, of spontaneous historical action, which in the long-run sustains, nourishes and impels human destinies."

We must dare to struggle and dare to win a nation in which neither the federal government or the collectivist dogma espoused by the New Leftist cabal is allowed to destroy the ever important struggle for individual rights and action.

It is absurd to contend that the current Left in the United States is not seeking some kind of power. Mao Tse-tung has written that "political power grows out of the barrel of a gun" and the youthful leftists seem determined to enact a self-fulfilling prophecy. The "crazies" are determined only to wreck the whole thing and seem incapable of realizing that once the structure is destroyed that "political power" will be imposed at the barrel of a gun.

A brief look at one of the New Left's intellectual mentors gives us a clue to the political character of these nihilists. Herbert Marcuse is an apparent idol of much of the existing leftist children. I cannot, because of space considerations, give a full analysis of the intellectual pitfalls of the Marcuse position and must instead only note a brief consideration recently made by Konrad Lorenz, the author of the brilliant study *On Aggression*, who said in an interview that "Marcuse is one of those utopian madmen who believe that it's possible to build from the ground up. He believes that if everything is destroyed, everything automatically regrows. It's a terrifying error. Marcuse does not really understand the mechanisms by which evolution and culture work in tandem and complement one another—nor did Karl Marx and Engels understand these mechanisms."

The so-called New Left has been apt at capturing the allegiance of many young people because it has operated on the two levels of idealism and fraud. Idealistically, this left-wing is an effective operation. If you are distressed with the general condition of society you are naturally drawn to a utopian solution. The left-wing holds out utopia in the form of socialism. Not a Cuban or Russian or Chinese socialism, but an American socialism. The left-wing socialism would not be like the socialism of Fidel or Stalin or Kim Il Sung. No, American socialism would be purely American, but it would still be socialism. I recall that we once asked Fidel Castro what advice he would give us for the "new American revolution." He immediately answered that he would not give us any advice because he was not an American - he was a Cuban. And just as he would not have accepted advice from us on how best to create a revolution in Cuba so we should not ask him to tell us how to create a revolution in America. It is high time that Americans realized that revolutions are not exportable commodities. If America ever turns to socialism it will not be because of Cuba or China. If we ever turn to socialism it will be because the government has become so disparaged in the public mind that a group of determined collectivist revolutionaries manage to wrench the power control from the hands of the two party administration then in power.

Youth has always been in revolt against some part of society. It is a natural impulse and it is good that young people doubt. We can easily see the results of a society in which people stop questioning and no longer value self over community. North Korea and Communist China are prime examples of what can happen when a society becomes one unto itself. I, for one, refuse to live in such a society and so I must support the right of the young to question.

But questioning does not mean destruction. The communists operating within the New Left movement sought the total transformation of society from the inception of the New Left. They have used the precept of idealism in order to whet the political appetites of the young. The Communists have said "trust us" and at some juncture in history we will have a totally free society. It sounds good, it is idealistic, it is almost real but there is a bug. And that bug is violence *and* the unspoken truth that only thru a centralized government can we ever hope to achieve this vaunted total freedom.

And so the left-wing has argued "trust us" *now* and at some point you will be free. Some of us fell for the line and have lived to regret it. Others, having better instincts, have known that man can not seek his individual freedom through total government control of his life.

The carrot-and-the-stick approach to political power has been with us since the inception of the state. Today, we are promised a bright future if we will only be willing to accept a little bit of socialist control.

The problem is obvious: once the collectivists (no matter what they title themselves they are the same generic beast, i.e., socialist, communist, fascist, yippies, etc.) get their foot in the door the product is more than half-sold. The collectivists have already gotten their foot in the door in this nation. I hardly need note the increasing tax burdens that we face or the growth of the governmental bureaucracy.

The left-wing holds out a promise of some future Nirvana. The statists hold out the same kind of promise but they utilize different slogans and media means. The point of the game for the left-wing has always been power. They believe that human misery can be cured if only they were granted the power to control human destiny. The Russians, the Chinese, the North Koreans, all believe that they have "God on their side." In this case, however, "God" is defined as history and economic production.

For the future of America, the question of what our citizens believe, and our leaders act upon, is the important point. I can not conceive of many Americans actually accepting the premises of communism through their own free will. The left-wing has operated on the assumption that man will not accept these premises through his own free will and therefore he must be subjugated through force.

The left-wing politicians have utilized every major social ill in our nation as a launching pad for their on-slaught against individualism. The New Left did not create the campus crisis but it utilized it once the objective conditions were ripe. The communists have never been able to take the specific social/economic/political problem and relate it to their goals.

We must dare to struggle and dare to win because man must be free to function as an individual. Hopefully, the New Left will degenerate under the intellectually fraudulent weight of collectivism and terrorism. But the nation today is being rent assunder in part because we as individuals have not dared to struggle against both the New Leftists and the ever growing governmental bureaucracy.

I am not a philosopher. I hold no alchemist stone. I return to Frank Chodorov and his monumental *Out of Step: the Autobiography of an Individualist:*

> "Of this, however, we can be sure: enrolled in some nursery or freshman class right now is a Voltaire, an Adam Smith, a John Locke or a Godwin, some maverick who will emerge from the herd and lead it to new pastures. Youth, as always, is in a ferment, is dissatisfied with things as they are. Well, since the only direction youth can go is away from the current collectivism toward its opposite, those who cherish the individualistic stock of values must try to peddle them to these embryonic revolutionists. We must polish up our ancient arguments, apply them to the current scene and offer them as brand new merchandise. We must do a selling job. Youth will not buy us out, lock, stock and barrel, but will be rather selective about it; they will take what seems good to them, modernize it, build it into a panacea and start a revolution. God bless them."

INDEX